SCRIPTURE
and the
ROSARY

NEW TESTAMENT MYSTERIES
OLD TESTAMENT PARALLELS

JENNIFER MCGAW PHELPS & TAMI PALLADINO

A CATHOLIC APPROACH TO SCRIPTURE

Printed by The Printery House
Conception Abbey
Conception, Missouri 64433

ISBN 978-0-615-65517-8

TABLE OF CONTENTS

CONTEMPLATING CHRIST WITH MARY

ROSARIUM VIRGINIS MARIAE: INTRODUCTION & CHAPTER 1

In *Rosarium Virginis Mariae* (The Rosary of the Virgin Mary), Blessed John Paul II (1920–2005) describes the Rosary as "a true doorway to the depths of the Heart of Christ, ocean of joy and of light, of suffering and of glory." A powerful prayer, the Rosary has changed history and continues to change the lives of countless men and women who regularly turn to it in times of extreme need, joy, or sorrow.

This prayer-based study begins with a look at the apostolic letter of 2002 that introduced the Luminous Mysteries of the Rosary. It examines key elements of the Creed as they relate to the Rosary, and it focuses on all 20 New Testament Mysteries with Old Testament parallels. The goal is to foster a deeper relationship with God through contemplation of the Rosary of the Blessed Virgin Mary.

Think about the people you know who regularly pray the Rosary. In what other ways do they demonstrate their faith? How were you first introduced to the Rosary? What is your favorite Mystery of the Rosary and why? Describe your most profound experience while praying the Rosary.

sac•ra•men•tals
sacred signs resembling the sacraments

The Rosary is one of the most popular **sacramentals**. Others include blessing with holy water, making pilgrimages, and praying the Stations of the Cross. Paragraph 1670 of the *Catechism of the Catholic Church* (CCC) teaches that, like sacraments, **sacramentals** draw their power from the Passion, death, and Resurrection of Christ. They prepare men and women to receive and cooperate with the grace of the Holy Spirit.

1 Introduction. In 2002 when Blessed John Paul II wrote *Rosarium Virginis Mariae,* he saw three concerns contributing to what he called a crisis of the Rosary: 1) The prayers were not being taught to young people; 2) it was feared by some that the Rosary was detracting from the liturgy of the Eucharist; and 3) because of its Marian character the Rosary was unacceptable to some Christians. Explain whether you think that these same issues are prevalent today.

2 A face radiant as the sun. In the Transfiguration Jesus appears in radiant glory, and the event itself can be seen as an icon of Christian contemplation. What does St. Paul promise is the result of beholding (or contemplating) the glory of Christ (see *2 Corinthians* 3:18)? Give an example of another Rosary Mystery that shows the divinity of Jesus shining through his humanity. (For a list of the Mysteries, see the *Table of Contents* on page 3.)

3 Mary, model of contemplation. Through the Mysteries of the Rosary, the Blessed Virgin Mary contemplates the face of Jesus in a variety of situations. With which of these scenes do you most closely identify, and why? What qualities do you think make Mary an "incomparable model" of contemplation of her Son, Jesus Christ?

ENCYCLICALS & APOSTOLIC LETTERS

A papal encyclical is a general letter from a pope about a particular topic. Primarily addressed to bishops, encyclicals also are meant for circulation among priests and laity. The title of an encyclical is in Latin and usually is taken from the first words, as in *Rosarium Virginis Mariae*, translated as "The Rosary of the Virgin Mary." The word encyclical is from Latin *encyclia*, meaning "general" or "encircling." An apostolic letter is similar to an encyclical, but it is less formal and is directed to all of the people of God. Apostolic letters and encyclicals pertaining to the Rosary can be found at **www.vatican.va.**

4 Mary's memories. *Luke* 2:19 records that the Blessed Virgin Mary pondered "in her heart" her memories related to Jesus' birth. What memories of Jesus do you treasure and hold in your heart? What do you think that pondering those memories involves?

5 The Rosary, a contemplative prayer. *Rosarium Virginis Mariae* points out the importance of contemplating the Mysteries of the Rosary instead of engaging in a mere "mechanical repetition" of them. What are some ways you can think of that might help to develop "a quiet rhythm and a lingering pace" when praying the Rosary?

6 Remembering Christ with Mary. Throughout Scripture memory is directly tied to worship—for example: "Remember the sabbath day, to keep it holy" (*Exodus* 20:8) and "Do this in remembrance of me" (*1 Corinthians* 11:24). How can praying the Mysteries of the Rosary based on events in Jesus' life enhance worship?

7 Learning Christ from Mary. Explain how Mary's response at the Annunciation reflects Jesus Christ (see *Luke* 1:38).

8 Being conformed to Christ with Mary. List some virtues in addition to perfection that can be learned by keeping company with Jesus and Mary through praying the Rosary. How does St. Louis de Montfort define perfection in connection with conformity to Christ?

9 Praying to Christ with Mary. What is the Church's response to the common misunderstanding that the Rosary is a prayer to Mary instead of a prayer to God (see *CCC* 2679 and *CCC* 2682)?

10 Proclaiming Christ with Mary. The Rosary long has been successfully used as a weapon against heresy. What do you think are the most serious heretical challenges faced by the contemporary Church, and how would you suggest increasing awareness of the power of the Rosary in overcoming evil in today's culture?

The Rosary is my favorite prayer. A marvelous prayer! Marvelous in its simplicity and its depth.

—Blessed John Paul II
16 October 2002

THE HEART OF THE ROSARY

At its heart, the Rosary is a contemplation of Jesus Christ. In it, Christians pray beside his Mother, the woman who knows and loves Jesus best. The Mysteries of the Rosary are Mary's key memories of her Son's life, with both its joys and sorrows.

Rosarium Virginis Mariae teaches: "The center of gravity in the *Hail Mary,* the hinge as it were which joins its two parts, is *the name of Jesus.* … It is precisely the emphasis given to the name of Jesus and to his mystery that is the sign of a meaningful and fruitful recitation of the Rosary."

The Rosary prayers begin and end with Jesus Christ. Rather than drawing devotion away from Jesus, the Rosary echoes Mary's Magnificat in which she praises God because her soul magnifies the Lord, and her spirit rejoices in God her Savior (*Luke* 1:46–47). The Rosary is a Christocentric prayer—that is, it is totally centered on Christ.

THE ROSARY: A COMPENDIUM OF THE GOSPEL

ROSARIUM VIRGINIS MARIAE: CHAPTER 2

A compendium is a brief summary of a larger work. The second chapter of *Rosarium Virginis Mariae* refers to the Rosary as a compendium of the Gospel, which means that it is a prayer that comprises key events in the life of Jesus Christ. When Christians pray the Rosary, meditating on all of its Mysteries, they cover the entire life, death, and Resurrection of Jesus and become immersed in the Gospel message, or the "good news" about Jesus. This path of prayer leads away from mere petitions and into a deeper and more intimate relationship with God. This in turn leads sincere believers into in a more loving relationship with all of the other people in their lives.

Explain which parts of the Gospel most relate to current experiences in your life or the life of someone you know. How are those particular Gospel scenes related to the Mysteries of the Rosary?

MORE FROM BLESSED JOHN PAUL II

For more information about how the mystery of Christ sheds light on the mystery of man, see the following writings:

- *Evengelium Vitae* (The Gospel of Life) 25 March 1995
- *Familiaris Consortio* (The Role of the Christian Family in the Modern World) 22 November 1981
- *Novo Millennio Ineunte* (Beginning of the New Millennium) 6 January 2001
- *Redemptor Hominis* (The Redeemer of Man) 4 March 1979
- *Redemptoris Mater* (Mother of the Redeemer) 25 March 1987
- *Salvifici Doloris* (The Christian Meaning of Human Suffering) 11 February 1984

1 A compendium of the Gospel. *Rosarium Virginis Mariae* strongly encourages attentive listening and silence in prayer in order to know and understand Jesus Christ. Paragraph 144 of the *Catechism of the Catholic Church* explains that hearing and listening are related to the obedience of faith, and it teaches that Mary is the most perfect embodiment of obedience offered in Scripture. Name one or two settings that you find conducive to listening to God. In what ways do you think that Jesus might be asking you to be more obedient?

2 A proposed addition to the traditional pattern. What Old Testament book serves as the pattern for the original prayers of the Rosary? What reason did Blessed John Paul II give for proposing the five new Mysteries, and what are those Mysteries? What other events in Jesus' life do you think might be fitting for contemplation?

3 The Joyful Mysteries. What is the key event from which all five of the Joyful Mysteries radiate? List some ways that Christians can reflect this event in the world. In what specific ways has Jesus brought joy into your life?

4 The Mysteries of Light. *Rosarium Virginis Mariae* teaches that each of the Mysteries of Light "is a revelation of the kingdom now present in the very person of Jesus." Explain how each one of the Luminous Mysteries reveals the divinity of Jesus Christ.

5 In *John* 1:34, John the Baptist identifies Jesus as the Son of God because this has been revealed to him by the Father. How does Mary's relationship with Jesus differ from John the Baptist's relationship with Jesus, and how does this affect Mary's understanding about who Jesus is? How is Mary's understanding reflected in her great maternal counsel: "Do whatever he tells you" (*John* 2:5)?

6 **The Sorrowful Mysteries.** Meditating on the suffering of Jesus reveals the depths of Gods' love for humanity. According to Church teaching, why did Jesus willingly undergo such suffering unto death (see *CCC* 609)? What type of power is imparted to Christians as a result of Jesus' suffering?

7 **The Glorious Mysteries.** How do each of the five Glorious Mysteries exhibit newness of life? How do they increase the Christian virtue of hope? In *Rosarium Virginis Mariae*, Pentecost is seen revealing the face of the Church as a family gathered together with Mary. How are you carrying out the mission of this family?

8 **Mary's Way.** *Rosarium Virginis Mariae* teaches that the Virgin of Nazareth possesses the "secret" that leads to a profound and inward knowledge of Christ. From what you know about Mary from Scripture, how does she exemplify faith, silence, and attentive listening, and in what ways do you feel called to follow her example?

9 **Mystery of Christ, mystery of man.** "Cast your burden on the LORD, and he will sustain you," *Psalm* 55:22 (*Psalm* 55:23 in the New American Bible [NAB]), encourages turning to God in time of need. Identify problems in your life. How can you set aside time to hand over these burdens to the hearts of Jesus and his Mother?

10 Rhythm is a regular repeated pattern of movement or sound. How does praying the Rosary conform your will to the will of God in order to bring your life into harmony with God's own life?

> *As a Gospel prayer, centered on the mystery of the redemptive Incarnation, the Rosary is a prayer with a clearly Christological orientation. Its most characteristic element, in fact, the litany-like succession of Hail Marys, becomes in itself an unceasing praise of Christ.*
>
> —Pope Paul VI
> 2 February 1974

duc in al•tum
put out into the deep

In *Rosarium Virginis Mariae*, Blessed John Paul II repeats Jesus' call to his disciples— **duc in altum**, "put out into the deep" (*Luke* 5:4)—a call that forms the basis of the apostolic letter, *Novo Millennio Ineunte* (Beginning of the New Millennium). Praying the Rosary allows Christians to continue to go ever deeper into the mystery of Christ, shining light on the human mystery: "Anyone who contemplates Christ through the various stages of his life cannot fail to perceive in him *the truth about man*."

FACE TO FACE WITH THE TRUTH

When Christians pray the Rosary, they meditate on the events of Jesus' life and accompany him on his path. Through this sharing in the Joyful Mysteries of Christ's Incarnation, the Luminous Mysteries revealing his divinity, the Sorrowful Mysteries of his salviific suffering, and the Glorious Mysteries of new and eternal life, men and women learn the truth about their own humanity.

Longing to see God is a major biblical theme. "My soul thirsts for God, for the living God. When shall I come and behold the face of God?" (*Psalm* 42:2 [*Psalm* 42:3 NAB]). "Philip said to [Jesus], 'Lord, show us the Father, and we shall be satisfied.' Jesus said to him, 'Have I been with you so long, and yet you do not know me, Philip? He who has seen me has seen the Father'" (*John* 14:8–9).

When we look at Jesus we see ourselves in his humanity, and in his divinity we see the goal toward which each of us is called, if we allow ourselves to be healed and transformed by the Holy Spirit.

ASSIMILATING THE MYSTERY OF CHRIST

ROSARIUM VIRGINIS MARIAE: CHAPTER 3 & CONCLUSION

One of the primary messages of *Rosarium Virginis Mariae* can be summed up in this quote: "Anyone who assimilates the mystery of Christ—and this is clearly the goal of the Rosary—learns the secret of peace and makes it his life project."

It is through the repetitive prayers of the Rosary that Christians learn Christ's way of peace at the knee of their Mother, the Blessed Virgin Mary. All children learn through repetition and example. We pick up habits of love and peace by participating in the prayer of the Christian family.

When life becomes especially challenging, it can be difficult to find the words for prayer. It is at such times that Christians can pick up their Rosaries as if holding their Mother's hand. She never tires of hearing her children say "I love you."

ART & PRAYER

In *Rosarium Virginis Mariae*, Blessed John Paul II encourages the use of icons and visual elements to help Christians focus and to assist them in entering more deeply into the meditation of each Mystery of the Rosary.

1 A way of assimilating the mystery. Assimilation means "to come to resemble." How does the repetition of the Hail Mary prayer in the Rosary serve as a method that men and women can use to come to resemble Jesus and his Mother?

2 A valid method which can nevertheless be improved. What do you think is the primary difference between praying the Rosary and the repetitive chanting associated with some African, Hawaiian, Native American, Buddhist, and other world religions?

3 Announcing each mystery. Blessed John Paul II teaches that the Mysteries of the Rosary essentially are similar to snapshots of the life of Christ, and he encourages praying the Rosary in a setting of prolonged recollection in order to draw the mind to a more expansive reflection on the rest of the Gospel. Describe what such a setting of prolonged recollection might look like for you.

4 Listening to the word of God. According to *Rosarium Virginis Mariae,* what benefits accrue from proclamation of a biblical passage related to the Mystery being prayed in the Rosary?

5 Silence. How do you think that listening and meditation are nourished or fed by silence? When does Blessed John Paul II encourage silence as the Rosary is being prayed? How can you create a silent place for prayer?

6 The prayers. According to Blessed John Paul II, why is it important to include the Our Father when praying the Rosary? How is this prayer ecclesial? What is the "greatest miracle of history" that Christians celebrate when praying the Hail Mary? Explain how praying the Glory Be at the end of each decade of the Rosary functions as the high point of contemplation. (For more information and a diagram about *How to Pray the Rosary*, see page 106.)

7 Peace. *Rosarium Virginis Mariae* was written in 2002. Explain whether you think that the same challenges to peace still plague the world. What might be some new challenges to peace? Read *Isaiah* 9:6–7 (*Isaiah* 9:5–6 NAB), which identifies the Messiah as the Prince of Peace. How does the peace promised by Isaiah differ from the peace offered by the world today? Why do you think that the Rosary has a peaceful effect on a person praying it?

8 The family. Just as Liturgy of the Hours, or the Prayer of the Church, is a path of contemplation for parish communities and Christian groups, so is the Rosary a complementary path, and especially recommended for families. In what specific ways does praying the Rosary as a family strengthen relationships? When was the last time your family prayed the Rosary? What are some creative ways that the Rosary can be presented to children and young people?

9 A treasure to be rediscovered. What group of Christians does Blessed John Paul II exclude from his appeal to take up the Rosary and rediscover it in the light of Scripture, in harmony with the liturgy, and in the context of daily life? How can you promote the Rosary in your circle of influence?

10 What are the most important things you have learned from Blessed John Paul II's apostolic letter about the Rosary? What can you do to help others discover or rediscover this "easy yet so rich" prayer? What plans can you make today to begin to pray the Rosary or to strengthen your habit of praying the Rosary?

> *Although the repeated Hail Mary is addressed directly to Mary, it is to Jesus that the act of love is ultimately directed, with her and through her. The repetition is nourished by the desire to be conformed ever more completely to Christ, the true program of the Christian life.*
>
> —Blessed John Paul II
> 16 October 2002

EXPRESSIONS OF PRAYER

Anyone serious about prayer would do well to read the section of the *Catechism of the Catholic Church* devoted to "Christian Prayer" (Part Four). The three major expressions of prayer found there are highlighted below. The Church teaches that they share one basic trait—composure of heart.

Vocal prayer. "Through his Word, God speaks to man. By words, mental or vocal, our prayer takes flesh" (*CCC* 2700). Involving the bodily senses in interior prayer corresponds to a requirement inherent in human nature. Men and women are body and spirit, and they must pray with their whole beings to give all power possible to their supplication.

Meditation. Defined as a quest of the mind to understand the why and how of Christian life, meditation requires attentiveness that can be difficult to sustain. Books and Scripture, particularly the Gospels, are especially helpful. "To meditate on what we read helps us to make it our own by confronting it with ourselves. Here, another book is opened: the book of life. To the extent that we are humble and faithful, we discover in meditation the movements that stir the heart" (*CCC* 2706).

Contemplation. The Church teaches that contemplative prayer is a gift, a grace; it is the intense time in which men and women are grounded in love; it is a gaze of faith, fixed on Jesus; it is hearing the Word of God through obedience of faith; it is silence, symbol of the world to come. Contemplative prayer is a union with the prayer of Christ insofar as it makes us participate in his mystery and manifests it in acts of love. (*CCC* 2712–*CCC* 2718).

LESSON 4

GOD THE FATHER: CREATION AND FAITH

The Apostles' Creed traditionally is prayed as an introduction to the Rosary. In the Creed, Christian believers profess faith in each person of the Blessed Trinity, beginning with God the Father, Creator of heaven and earth.

The primary panel of this stained glass window depicts God's act of Creation. It is paired with a representation of the theological virtue of faith, exemplified in the Old Testament by the actions of the patriarch Abraham.

In the Creation account in *Genesis* 1:26–31, God blesses Adam and Eve and instructs them to be fruitful. The principal Rosary prayer, the Hail Mary, celebrates the Blessed Virgin Mary and praises God's fruitfulness in her life.

List some specific blessings that God has given you. In what ways do you consider your life to be fruitful?

For what purpose do you think that you were created, and do you feel that you are living out God's plan for your life? What might God pronounce "very good" when looking at you?

GENESIS 1:26–31

²⁶Then God said, "Let us make man in our image, after our likeness; and let them have dominion over the fish of the sea, and over the birds of the air, and over the cattle, and over all the earth, and over every creeping thing that creeps upon the earth." ²⁷So God created man in his own image, in the image of God he created him; male and female he created them. ²⁸And God blessed them, and God said to them, "Be fruitful and multiply, and fill the earth and subdue it; and have dominion over the fish of the sea and over the birds of the air and over every living thing that moves upon the earth." ²⁹And God said, "Behold, I have given you every plant yielding seed which is upon the face of all the earth, and every tree with seed in its fruit; you shall have them for food. ³⁰And to every beast of the earth, and to every bird of the air, and to everything that creeps on the earth, everything that has the breath of life, I have given every green plant for food." And it was so. ³¹And God saw everything that he had made, and behold, it was very good.

THE APOSTLES' CREED

I believe in God,
   the Father almighty,
   Creator of heaven and earth.
and in Jesus Christ,
   his only Son, our Lord.
   who was conceived
   by the Holy Spirit,
   born of the Virgin Mary.
   suffered under Pontius Pilate,
   was crucified, died,
   and was buried.
   he descended into hell;
   on the third day he rose again
   from the dead;
he ascended into heaven,
   and is seated at the right hand
   of God the Father almighty.
   from there he will come to
   judge the living and the dead.
I believe in the Holy Spirit,
   the holy catholic Church,
   the communion of saints,
   the forgiveness of sins,
   the resurrection of the body,
   and life everlasting. Amen.

The Apostles' Creed summarizes the faith and is the ancient baptismal symbol of the Church of Rome. Its Christian authority arises from this fact. Paragraph 194 of the *Catechism of the Catholic Church* teaches that it is "the Creed of the Roman Church, the See of Peter, the first of the apostles, to which he brought the common faith."

1 In Scripture, all three persons of the Blessed Trinity take an active part in Creation. Explain the role of each—God the Father, Jesus the Son, and the Holy Spirit (see *Genesis* 1:1–2 and *John* 1:1–3).

2 Paragraph 760 of the *Catechism of the Catholic Church* teaches: "The world was created for the sake of the Church." How do you see God creatively working within the Church today to bring about communion with the divine life of the Blessed Trinity?

3 The blood-red blossom on the tree of the knowledge of good and evil represents both the fruitfulness of God's blessing of Adam and Eve, recorded in *Genesis* 1:28, and the growth of future problems for humanity related to eating forbidden fruit. The sinuous curves of foliage hint at the cunning serpent to come. What sin do Adam and Eve commit? Who is the serpent, and what is his role in the fall of humanity (see *Genesis* 3:1–7 and *CCC* 397)? How does the Church explain the transmission of original sin (see *CCC* 404)?

4 *Genesis* 3:8–20 recounts events in the Garden of Eden following the fall of humanity. One verse, *Genesis* 3:15, is called the *protoevangelium,* or first good news, because it is considered the first announcement of the Gospel to be found in Scripture. How is the Blessed Virgin Mary depicted in the Creation window? Explain her role in God's plan for the salvation of men and women.

5 In contrast to the tree of the knowledge of good and evil, a cross appears at the top of the stained glass window. Discuss how the cross of Christ can be understood as a symbol of the tree of life.

Sa•cred Te•tra•gram•ma•ton
four Hebrew letters that form the proper name of God

In the stained glass window, Adam and Eve gaze at a triangular representation of the Blessed Trinity known as the **Sacred Tetragrammaton.** God the Father is indicated by outstretched arms, and Jesus Christ, the second person of the Trinity, is symbolized by the Hebrew letters for Adonai (LORD in many translations of the Bible). The stylized scallops represent a cloud of mystery, one of several images of the Holy Spirit used in art.

HUMANITY'S JOURNEY TOWARD GOD

The Garden of Eden often is thought to represent perfection. This contradicts Church teaching, which holds that while Creation has its own goodness, it did not spring forth complete from the hands of the Creator. Instead, the world and everything in it was created "in a state of journeying" toward the ultimate perfection to which God has destined it (*CCC* 302). About this mystery, St. Thomas Aquinas (1225–1274) wrote: "There is nothing to prevent human nature's being raised up to something greater, even after sin."

GENESIS XVIII:2

Abraham kneels before three mysterious visitors.

GENESIS 18:2–5, 8–10

²[Abraham] lifted up his eyes and looked, and behold, three men stood in front of him. When he saw them, he ran from the tent door to meet them, and bowed himself to the earth, ³and said, "My lord, if I have found favor in your sight, do not pass by your servant. ⁴Let a little water be brought, and wash your feet, and rest yourselves under the tree, ⁵while I fetch a morsel of bread, that you may refresh yourselves, and after that you may pass on—since you have come to your servant." So they said, "Do as you have said." … ⁸Then he took curds, and milk, and the calf which he had prepared, and set it before them; and he stood by them under the tree while they ate.

⁹They said to him, "Where is Sarah your wife?" And he said, "She is in the tent." ¹⁰The LORD said, I will surely return to you in the spring, and Sarah your wife shall have a son."

OUR FATHER ABRAHAM

The Old Testament parallel to Creation is a representation of the theological, or supernatural, virtue of faith viewed in connection with God's promise to give a son to Abram (who is renamed Abraham in *Genesis* 17:5). Scripture alludes to the mysterious nature of the trio who appear to the patriarch by alternately referring to them in the singular and the plural, and they have come to be known as the "Old Testament Trinity."

During their visit, the three announce that Abraham's aging wife, Sarah, soon will bear the son promised by God (*Genesis* 12:1–2, *Genesis* 13:14–16, and *Genesis* 15:4–5). Such fruitfulness reinforces the theme of Creation by drawing attention to the idea of fatherhood, the most common image of God. Abraham's fatherhood is linked to his faith; Scripture records that he was 100 years old when Isaac was born (*Genesis* 21:5).

The author of the *Letter to the Hebrews* lauds Sarah for her faith as well, and points out that Abraham's large number of descendants is connected to his great faith in God's word. The Church sees Abraham as a model of obedience (*CCC* 144).

Pairing the Old Testament announcement of a son to be born to Abraham with God's Creation of the world emphasizes the image of God as a Father and points to the role that God's only begotten Son, Jesus Christ, will play in freeing men and women from bondage to sin and death.

6 Abraham is an Old Testament patriarch, a word that means father, and he is considered the "father of all who believe." In *Genesis* 12:1, how do you think that Abraham is able to recognize the voice of the LORD telling him to leave his home and family?

7 A Creation parallel is seen in the story of the "Old Testament Trinity" who tell good news to Abraham. What is this news (*Genesis* 18:2–10), and how might it be related to the good news of the Gospel?

8 Paragraph 144 of the *Catechism of the Catholic Church* teaches: "To obey in faith is to submit freely to the word that has been heard, because its truth is guaranteed by God, who is Truth itself." Why do you think that Abraham is considered a model of obedience (see *Genesis* 12:1—22:19)? Explain why the Church sees the Blessed Virgin Mary as the most perfect embodiment of obedience. In what ways does obedience to God play a role in your own life of faith?

9 In the *Letter to the Hebrews* 11:8–12, Abraham's wife Sarah is lauded for her faith. What does the author of this letter see happening as the result of Abraham and Sarah's faith, and how does this fulfill God's promises to Abraham (see *Genesis* 12:1–2, *Genesis* 13:14–16, and *Genesis* 15:4–5)?

10 Read paragraphs 222—227 of the *Catechism of the Catholic Church*. What consequences does faith in God have in the lives of Christians? How do you see these at work in your own life?

> ❝ The Church always has considered the act of entrusting oneself to God to be a moment of fundamental decision which engages the whole person. In that act, the intellect and the will display their spiritual nature, enabling the subject to act in a way which realizes personal freedom to the full. It is not just that freedom is part of the act of faith; it is absolutely required. Indeed, it is faith that allows individuals to give consummate expression to their own freedom.… Men and women can accomplish no more important act in their lives than the act of faith. It is here that freedom reaches the certainty of truth and chooses to live in that truth. ❞ —*Fides et Ratio* (The Relationship Between Faith and Reason)

IN THE BEGINNING

The Apostles' Creed contains the essential Christian beliefs about God, and it begins with the profession that God is the Creator of heaven and earth. Paragraph 326 of the *Catechism of the Catholic Church* teaches: "The Scriptural expression 'heaven and earth' means all that exists, creation in its entirety. It also indicates the bond, deep within creation, that both unites heaven and earth and distinguishes the one from the other: 'the earth' is the world of men, while 'heaven' or 'the heavens' can designate both the firmament and God's own 'place'—'our Father in heaven.'…"

God the Father, Jesus the Son, and the Holy Spirit all appear in the triangular representation of the Blessed Trinity in the stained glass window dedicated to God the Father (*page 10*), a visualization of the presence of all three at Creation.

The three persons also can be seen in the account of Creation in *Genesis* 1:1–3: "In the beginning God created the heavens and the earth. The earth was without form and void, and darkness was upon the face of the deep, and the Spirit of God was moving over the face of the waters. And God said, 'Let there be light'; and there was light."

In the window, double images of a dove depict the Holy Spirit in motion over the face of the waters, which are seen below the earth at the feet of Adam and Eve. Jesus, the Word of God and light of the world, is seen in the Hebrew word for LORD in the Sacred Tetragrammaton above the sky.

The Church considers the Most Holy Trinity to be the central mystery of Christian faith and life because it is the mystery of God in himself and therefore the source of all other mysteries of the faith.

GOD'S ONLY SON: REDEMPTION AND HOPE

The Redemption Window focuses on Jesus as the Son of God, which is emphasized in the middle section of the Apostles' Creed (*page 11*). The Redemption Window also illustrates the corresponding theological virtue of hope.

The anchor at the top of the window incorporates the shape of a cross, and an anchor is the traditional symbol of Christian hope that is based on the redemption of humanity brought about by Jesus' Passion, death, and Resurrection. It is because of Jesus' willingness to die in expiation for the sins of the world that men and women now are able to share in the promise of eternal life. Christians have only to seize the hope that is offered and cling to the cross as the anchor of their immortal souls.

The opposite of hope is despair. The epidemic of depression in the world is an indicator of underlying despair. Think of people you know who are in danger of becoming overwhelmed by despair. What specific difficulties do they face that are contributing to their lack of hope? What difficulties threaten to overwhelm the contemporary world? What difficulties challenge you in your own life? Ask God to show you how to bring about an increase of hope in your life and in the world.

HEBREWS 6:13–20

[13]For when God made a promise to Abraham, since he had no one greater by whom to swear, he swore by himself, [14]saying, "Surely I will bless you and multiply you." [15]And thus Abraham, having patiently endured, obtained the promise. [16]Men indeed swear by a greater than themselves, and in all their disputes an oath is final for confirmation. [17]So when God desired to show more convincingly to the heirs of the promise the unchangeable character of his purpose, he interposed with an oath, [18]so that through two unchangeable things, in which it is impossible that God should prove false, we who have fled for refuge might have strong encouragement to seize the hope set before us. [19]We have this as a sure and steadfast anchor of the soul, a hope that enters into the inner shrine behind the curtain, [20]where Jesus has gone as a forerunner on our behalf, having become a high priest for ever according to the order of Melchizedek.

1 Paragraph 457 of the *Catechism of the Catholic Church* teaches that the first of four reasons for the Incarnation of Jesus Christ is to save humanity by reconciling men and women with God. From what did men and women need to be saved? What are the other three reasons for the Incarnation (see *CCC* 458—*CCC* 460)? Why do you think that reconciliation with God is listed as the first reason?

2 St. Irenaeus (130–202) wrote of the Blessed Virgin Mary: "Being obedient, she became the cause of salvation for herself and for the whole human race." To whom was Mary obedient? Explain how her obedience led to salvation for herself and all humanity.

3 What did Jesus sacrifice in order to bring about the redemption of humanity? Why was no one else able to make such a sacrifice for the good of all men and women (see *CCC* 616)? Explain ways in which Mary's obedience and Jesus' sacrifice are related.

4 *Genesis* 3:20 records that Adam called his wife's name Eve, "because she was the mother of all living." The early Church fathers referred to the Blessed Virgin Mary as the "new Eve" and as "the Mother of the living." Explain how Mary and Eve are similar, and compare that with the ways in which they differ.

5 Paragraph 605 of the *Catechism of the Catholic Church* teaches: "There is not, never has been, and never will be a single human being for whom Christ did not suffer." Explain how this understanding of Jesus as Redeemer is linked to the theological virtue of hope.

THEOLOGICAL VIRTUES

In the three stained glass windows that represent the Apostles' Creed, the theological virtues of faith, hope, and love (a virtue also called charity) correspond to God the Father, God the Son, and God the Holy Spirit. These virtues are theological because they dispose Christians to live in relationship with the Blessed Trinity. Paragraph 1813 of the *Catechism of the Catholic Church* teaches that these theological virtues give life to all the moral virtues: "They are infused by God into the souls of the faithful to make them capable of acting as his children and of meriting eternal life. They are the pledge of the presence and action of the Holy Spirit in the faculties of the human being."

THE THRONE OF WISDOM

Although the stained glass window on the opposite page emphasizes the role of the Son of God as Redeemer of humanity, the Blessed Virgin Mary appears prominently in its primary panel, which is patterned after the famous *Notre Dame de la Belle Verrière* (Our Lady of the Beautiful Window) in Chartres Cathedral in France. That window, a rare Romanesque panel surviving from 1150, was inspired in turn by Chartre's most notable relic, the *Sancta Camisa* (Sacred Veil), said to be the tunic worn by Mary at the birth of Jesus.

The throne upon which Mary is seated rests on the Temple of the new Jerusalem, which in turn rests on clouds of heaven. Mary herself forms the throne upon which Jesus sits, and this classic artistic composition is known as *Sedes Sapientia* (Throne of Wisdom). Both the Blessed Virgin Mary and the child Jesus wear crowns, and with his right hand Jesus imparts a blessing. In his left hand, Jesus holds a globe topped by a cross, symbolizing his role as redeemer of the world.

The Council of Ephesus in 431 proclaimed Mary the Mother of God, "not that the nature of the Word or his divinity received the beginning of its existence from the holy Virgin, but that, since the holy body, animated by a rational soul, which the Word of God united to himself…was born from her, the Word is said to be born according to the flesh."

In consenting to give birth to the Savior, Mary cooperated with God's plan, setting in motion the hope of salvation through events that ultimately would lead to the redemption of sinful humanity.

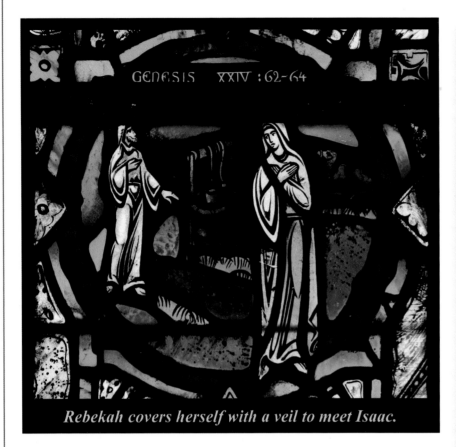
Rebekah covers herself with a veil to meet Isaac.

GENESIS 24:58–60, 62–67

⁵⁸And [Laban and Bethuel] called Rebekah, and said to her, "Will you go with this man?" She said, "I will go." ⁵⁹So they sent away Rebekah their sister and her nurse, and Abraham's servant and his men. ⁶⁰And they blessed Rebekah, and said to her, "Our sister, be the mother of thousands of ten thousands; and may your descendants possess the gate of those who hate them!"…

⁶²Now Isaac had come from Beerlahairoi, and was dwelling in the Negeb. ⁶³And Isaac went out to meditate in the field in the evening; and he lifted up his eyes and looked, and behold, there were camels coming. ⁶⁴And Rebekah lifted up her eyes, and when she saw Isaac, she alighted from the camel, ⁶⁵and said to the servant, "Who is the man yonder, walking in the field to meet us?" The servant said, "It is my master." So she took her veil and covered herself. ⁶⁶And the servant told Isaac all the things that he had done. ⁶⁷Then Isaac brought her into the tent, and took Rebekah, and she became his wife; and he loved her. So Isaac was comforted after his mother's death.

ISAAC: THE HEIR OF GOD'S PROMISE

In the Old Testament, Isaac can be seen as a prefiguration of Jesus Christ, God's beloved Son and Savior of the world. As the heir promised to Abraham by God, Abraham's willingness to sacrifice his son at God's request (*Genesis* 22:1–14) reinforces Abraham's role as our strong father in the faith.

As the intended victim of the sacrifice, Isaac becomes a type of Jesus, Son of God the Father. The author of the *Letter to the Hebrews* writes: "By faith Abraham, when he was tested, offered up Isaac, and he who had received the promises was ready to offer up his only-begotten son, of whom it was said, 'Through Isaac shall your descendants be named.' He considered that God was able to raise men even from the dead; hence he did receive him back and this was a symbol" (*Hebrews* 11:17–19).

As a result of Abraham's willingness to sacrifice his beloved son, God promises to bless Abraham, multiply his descendants, and make them a blessing to all the nations of the earth (*Genesis* 22:16–18).

In the New Testament, Jesus fulfills all of the Old Testament promises made by God to Abraham. Through his sacrificial death, Jesus fulfills his Father's will and institutes the new, eternal covenant. This covenant redeems sinful humanity and promises eternal life to those men and women willing to place all of their hope in Jesus Christ.

6 In the *Letter to the Hebrews* 6:19–20, the image of an anchor is used to describe Christian hope. Why do you think that the author chose that image, which suggests other images such as a boat and the sea. What do you think these other images might represent?

7 Read the story of the patriarch Abraham's willingness to sacrifice his son, Isaac (see *Genesis* 22:1–18). List ways that Abraham resembles God the Father and ways that Isaac resembles Jesus Christ. What reason does the author of the *Letter to the Hebrews* give for why Abraham was able to be so obedient when he consented to sacrifice his son Isaac (see *Hebrews* 11:19)?

8 In order for Abraham to have numerous descendants, it is necessary for Isaac to marry and have children. Abraham asks a trusted servant to choose a wife for his son. What sign does the servant seek in order to identify Isaac's bride (see *Genesis* 24:10–14)?

9 Isaac is seen as a type of Christ, who in the New Testament is referred to as a bridegroom by John the Baptist (see *John* 3:28–29), and by Jesus (see *Mark* 2:19). Who is the bride of Christ, and how is she chosen (see *Revelation* 19:7–8 and *Revelation* 22:17)?

10 Paragraph 1641 of the *Catechism of the Catholic Church* teaches that marriage is a sacred relationship between a man and a woman, intended to strengthen their unity and to welcome and educate children through openness to life. Explain how unity and increased life result from the marriage between Jesus and the Church.

> **❝** Man is redeemed by love…. If this absolute love exists, with its absolute certainty, then—only then—is man "redeemed"… whatever should happen to him in his particular circumstances. This is what it means to say: Jesus Christ has "redeemed" us. Through him we have become certain of God, a God who is not a remote "first cause" of the world, because his only-begotten Son has become man and everyone can say: "I live by faith in the Son of God, who loved me and gave himself for me" (*Galatians* 2:20). In this sense it is true that anyone who does not know God, even though he may entertain all kinds of hopes, is ultimately without hope, without the great hope that sustains the whole of life. **❞** —*Spe Salvi* (Christian Hope)

BRIDEGROOM & BRIDE: CHRIST & HIS CHURCH

The Redemption Window looks at a key scene in the life of Isaac, Abraham's son who is spared from a sacrificial death. In order for God to fulfill his promise to give Abraham numerous descendants, it is necessary for Isaac to become a father. Isaac's wife, Rebekah, is chosen for him by a trusted servant of his own father.

The window that shows Isaac's first meeting with Rebekah includes a well, indicating the extraordinary circumstances that surround Rebekah becoming Isaac's wife (*Genesis* 24:1–27).

The depiction of the well introduces the idea of covenantal fulfillment, a common Old Testament theme. It is only after Isaac has dug a series of wells that the LORD appears to him at Beersheba and renews with him the promises originally made to Abraham (*Genesis* 26:24–25).

Isaac clearly is a type of Jesus, and the ideas of marriage and covenantal fulfillment seen in

his marriage to Rebekah can be viewed as a foreshadowing of New Testament events.

The Old Testament describes the longing of God's people for a Messiah. The people of Israel represent a bride longing for a bridegroom. In Scripture, John the Baptist refers to Jesus as the bridegroom and to himself as the bridegroom's friend (*John* 3:28–29), and Jesus refers to himself as a bridegroom (*Mark* 2:19). The Apostle Paul describes the Church as a bride betrothed to Christ (*2 Corinthians* 11:2 and *Ephesians* 5:23–27). And the author of the book of *Revelation* also understands the Church to be the bride of Christ (*Revelation* 19:7–8 and *Revelation* 22:17).

Paragraph 796 of *Catechism of the Catholic Church* teaches that this imagery expresses the unity of Jesus Christ and his Church while also implying "the distinction of the two within a personal relationship."

THE HOLY SPIRIT: SANCTIFICATION AND LOVE

Sanctification, or holiness, is the primary theme of the window related to the Holy Spirit, the third person of the Most Blessed Trinity. The Sanctification Window is the last of the windows devoted to the Apostles' Creed (*page 11*), which is prayed as an introduction to the Mysteries of the Rosary.

The heart at the pinnacle of this window emphasizes the essential link between sanctification and love.

St. Thérèse of Lisieux (1873–1897) saw eternal love alone as the motivating force that enables all members of the Church to act: "If love ceased to function, apostles would forget to preach the Gospel, and martyrs would refuse to shed their blood."

Think of the person in your life who most exemplifies Christian love. Where else do you see love and holiness burning in the Church today? What do you love most about the Church? Ask God to help you bring more love into the world.

1 CORINTHIANS 13:1–10, 12–13

[1]If I speak in the tongues of men and of angels, but have not love, I am a noisy gong or a clanging cymbal. [2]And if I have prophetic powers, and understand all mysteries and all knowledge, and if I have all faith, so as to remove mountains, but have not love, I am nothing. [3]If I give away all I have, and if I deliver my body to be burned, but have not love, I gain nothing.

[4]Love is patient and kind; love is not jealous or boastful; [5]it is not arrogant or rude. Love does not insist on its own way; it is not irritable or resentful; [6]it does not rejoice at wrong, but rejoices in the right. [7]Love bears all things, believes all things, hopes all things, endures all things.

[8]Love never ends; as for prophecies, they will pass away; as for tongues, they will cease; as for knowledge, it will pass away. [9]For our knowledge is imperfect and our prophecy is imperfect; [10]but when the perfect comes, the imperfect will pass away....[12]For now we see in a mirror dimly, but then face to face. Now I know in part; then I shall understand fully, even as I have been understood. [13]So faith, hope, love abide, these three; but the greatest of these is love.

1 The image of the Blessed Virgin Mary kneeling before the Trinity is a fitting introduction to the Rosary. Paragraph 2708 of the *Catechism of the Catholic Church* teaches that "knowledge of the love of the Lord Jesus" is the goal of meditating on the mysteries of Christ. How does your favorite Rosary Mystery demonstrate God's love? (For a list of the Mysteries, see the *Table of Contents* on page 3.)

2 List as many means of sanctification (attaining holiness) as you can and explain how each is related to love. Describe how the Holy Spirit is active in each means of sanctification on your list.

3 The ultimate goal of humanity is entry into the perfect unity of the Blessed Trinity. Paragraph 260 of the *Catechism of the Catholic Church* teaches that even in this lifetime, each Christian is called to be a dwelling for the Most Holy Trinity. According to Jesus, how does this happen (see *John* 17:21–23)?

4 In his *First Letter to the Corinthians* 13:4–7, St. Paul provides a list of distinguishing qualities of love. Explain which quality you think is most needed in the world. What specific things can you do to bring about an increase of love in your workplace or family?

5 St. Paul writes that "when the perfect comes, the imperfect will pass away" (*1 Corinthians* 13:10). To what do you think that he is referring? According to St. Paul, what benefits will accrue when this perfection occurs (see *1 Corinthians* 13:12)?

> **❝** What is charity? St. Paul answers by giving a great number of properties of it, all distinct and special. In one sense charity is all virtues at once, and therefore St. Paul cannot describe it more definitely, more restrictedly than he does. In other words, it is the root of all holy dispositions, and grows and blossoms into them: They are its parts; and when it is described, they of necessity are mentioned. Love is the material (so to speak) out of which all graces are made, the quality of mind which is the fruit of regeneration, and in which the Spirit dwells. Faith and hope are graces of an imperfect state; but love is greater, because it is perfection. **❞**
> —from a homily by Blessed John Henry Newman

LOVE THAT NEVER ENDS

The Sanctification Window depicts God the Father in human likeness, something relatively rare in religious art. This is fitting, because it is through the Father's plan that humanity is restored to the likeness of God in his Son, Jesus Christ (*CCC* 705).

The Father is shown holding a scepter of power, and a triangular halo, or nimbus, appears behind him. He wears a crown and shares the throne of heaven with his Son. Jesus, seated at his Father's right, imparts a blessing. Father and Son together hold the world in their hands.

The third person of the Most Holy Trinity, the Holy Spirit, hovers above as a dove with rays of love extending outward. St. Paul describes how the gift of the love of God is transferred to men and women: "God's love has been poured into our hearts through the Holy Spirit who has been given

to us" (*Romans* 5:5). "The communion of the Holy Spirit in the Church restores to the baptized the divine likeness lost through sin" (*CCC* 734).

The presence of the Blessed Virgin Mary kneeling before Father, Son, and Holy Spirit can be interpreted as a sign that the kingdom of heaven now is open to humanity. It also reinforces the idea of God's burning love for all men and women. The Church teaches that Mary "is the burning bush of the definitive theophany" who manifests the Son of the Father to make God's Word visible in flesh (*CCC* 724).

It is through Mary's cooperation that the Holy Spirit is able to bring men and women into communion with the Most Holy Trinity. The mission of Jesus the Son and of the Holy Spirit then can be brought to completion in the Church.

Joseph embraces his father Jacob in Egypt.

IN THE LINE OF THE PATRIARCHS

The emotional reunion between Joseph and his father Jacob (Israel) is the theme of the Old Testament panel in the Sanctification Window. Many details in the scriptural account of Joseph's life make this scene an appropriate choice. Foremost, of course, is the love Jacob has for Joseph, his favorite son (*Genesis* 37:3).

Despite Joseph's special standing with his father, Joseph's brothers sell him into slavery in Egypt, where he manages to rise to great power. After Joseph saves his family and all of Egypt from serious famine, the family moves to Egypt. It is significant that Joseph asks for his remains to be carried back to the Promised Land when the family is able to return there in 400 years (*Genesis* 50:24–25). Joseph eventually is buried with his forefathers at Shechem (*Joshua* 24:32). This establishes him as an ancestor of much importance.

Joseph's status among his brothers is fixed when Jacob adopts and blesses Ephraim and Manasseh, and divides Joseph's inheritance between the two boys, born of Egyptian mothers (*Genesis* 48:8–22). Joseph himself appears to be bypassed, but that is, in fact, an indicator of his special standing before God. Joseph is the favorite son of Jacob, who in turn is the favorite son of Isaac, heir of the promise. After his death, Joseph goes to join the patriarchs—Abraham, Isaac, and Jacob.

GENESIS 46:26–30

[26]All the persons belonging to Jacob who came into Egypt, who were his own offspring, not including Jacob's sons' wives, were sixty-six persons in all; [27]and the sons of Joseph, who were born to him in Egypt, were two; all the persons of the house of Jacob, that came into Egypt, were seventy.

[28]He sent Judah before him to Joseph, to appear before him in Goshen; and they came into the land of Goshen. [29]Then Joseph made ready his chariot and went up to meet Israel his father in Goshen; and he presented himself to him, and fell on his neck, and wept on his neck a good while. [30]Israel said to Joseph, "Now let me die, since I have seen your face and know that you are still alive."

6 Paragraph 724 of the *Catechism of the Catholic Church* teaches that Mary is "the burning bush of the definitive theophany." A theophany is a visual manifestation of God. What role does the burning bush play in salvation history (see *Exodus* 3:1-10)? Why is this a fitting description of Mary? How is the Holy Spirit involved?

7 In the New Testament, the Blessed Virgin Mary's husband is named Joseph. Interesting parallels exist between him and his Old Testament namesake. The Joseph in *Genesis* 37:5–11 is described as a person who has prophetic dreams. How do prophetic dreams play a role in the life of the Joseph of the New Testament (see *Matthew* 1:18–25 and *Matthew* 2:13–14)?

8 In the Old Testament, Joseph's prophetic dreams are a factor in his brothers' jealousy. Where is Joseph taken after his brothers sell him into slavery, and what worse fate than slavery were the brothers considering for him (see *Genesis* 37:12–28)?

9 In addition to other similarities, the Josephs of the Old and New Testaments both have fathers named Jacob. In the Old Testament, Joseph and his brothers are direct descendants of Abraham, Isaac, and Jacob. *Genesis* 49:28–32 describes the final resting place of those patriarchs. Which one of the 12 sons of Jacob also is buried at that site (see *Joshua* 24:32)? *Joseph*

10 Paragraph 61 of the *Catechism of the Catholic Church* teaches that the patriarchs, prophets, and certain other Old Testament figures are honored as saints by the Church, which means that they can serve as examples of holiness for Christians. How does the relationship between Joseph and Jacob exemplify divine love?

---

sanc•ti•fi•ca•tion
being set apart for a sacred purpose; holiness

Sanctification is the process of being made holy. In Christianity, **sanctification** includes being cleansed from sin. Consecration often is used interchangeably with **sanctification**, but the word consecration typically implies a ceremonial liturgical act.

JOSEPH IN THE NEW TESTAMENT

Joseph's favored status in his father's eyes is alluded to in the New Testament. The genealogy in *Matthew* 1:1–16 indicates that Jesus' earthly father is named Joseph, and he, in turn, is the son of a man named Jacob. This genealogy places Jesus squarely in the line of the Old Testament patriarchs, and it highlights Jesus as the fulfillment of God's promises to those patriarchs.

COLORS HELP TELL THE STORIES

The vibrant colors used in stained glass church windows are a distinguishing feature of this type of religious art. These colors do more than add visual interest, however. Each color— and even plain white—often is used symbolically. Knowing the traditional meanings of the different colors can aid in understanding more about the biblical scenes depicted.

White usually denotes purity, and it is used for Mary's veil. It also is the color of the Transfiguration.

Gold symbolizes the radiance of the divine presence, the glory of God, and also can indicate spiritual riches.

Green indicates spiritual growth and renewal, but sometimes can represent the presence of evil.

Red is the color of blood and fire. It depicts Jesus' Passion and the Holy Spirit's tongues of flame at Pentecost.

Blue, the color of the sky and of water, is used to denote heavenly backgrounds. It is the traditional color of the Blessed Virgin's mantle.

THE ANGEL GABRIEL WAS SENT TO A VIRGIN

The Annunciation Window depicts the archangel Gabriel telling the Blessed Virgin Mary that she has been chosen to become the mother of the long-awaited Messiah. The Annunciation is seen by the Church as a pivotal moment in the history of God's relationship with his people. Scripture indicates that it was through the grace of the Holy Spirit that Mary was given courage to respond to God's call.

Mary traditionally is believed to have been well educated in her Jewish faith, and she is shown kneeling before the Hebrew Scriptures (the Old Testament). What expectations do you bring to your study of Scripture? How do you think an increased understanding of the scriptural basis of the Rosary might affect your prayer life? *Use it often & frequently*

meaning

LUKE 1:26–35

[26]In the sixth month the angel Gabriel was sent from God to a city of Galilee named Nazareth, [27]to a virgin betrothed to a man whose name was Joseph, of the house of David; and the virgin's name was Mary. [28]And he came to her and said, "Hail, full of grace, the Lord is with you!" [29]But she was greatly troubled at the saying, and considered in her mind what sort of greeting this might be. [30]And the angel said to her, "Do not be afraid, Mary, for you have found favor with God. [31]And behold, you will conceive in your womb and bear a son, and you shall call his name Jesus.

[32]He will be great, and will be called the Son
    of the Most High;
and the Lord God will give to him the throne
    of his father David,
[33]and he will reign over the house of Jacob for ever;
and of his kingdom there will be no end."
[34]And Mary said to the angel, "How can this be, since I have no husband?" [35]And the angel said to her,
"The Holy Spirit will come upon you,
and the power of the Most High will overshadow you;
Therefore the child to be born will be called holy,
the Son of God."

1 The Marian dogma of the Immaculate Conception, proclaimed by Pope Pius IX in 1854, states: "The most Blessed Virgin Mary was, from the first moment of her conception, by a singular grace and privilege of almighty God and by virtue of the merits of Jesus Christ, Savior of the human race, preserved immune from all stain of original sin." What is original sin (refer to Question 3 in *God the Father: Creation & Faith* on page 11)? Which sacrament removes original sin for Christians (see *CCC* 405)? What does that sacrament have in common with way that Mary was preserved free from all stain of original sin? How does it differ?

2 According to Church teaching, what role does grace play throughout the course of Mary's life (see *CCC* 493)? In what ways do you think that this is appropriate for the Mother of God?

3 The Immaculate Conception frequently is misunderstood to refer to the virginal birth of Jesus. This leads to another common misunderstanding, that of equating sex with sin. Which sacrament provides for and promotes physical intimacy, and under what circumstances (see *CCC* 2360 and *CCC* 2361)?

4 In the Annunciation Window, the archangel Gabriel extends a while lily, a traditional symbol of purity, to Mary, who is a model of chastity in the Church. Explain the difference between virginal purity and Mary's preservation from the stain of original sin.

---

mys•ter•y
a religious belief based on divine revelation

In Catholic theology, **mystery** describes a Christian belief once regarded as beyond human understanding. In connection with the Rosary, **Mystery** refers to an incident in the life of Jesus. The Rosary **Mysteries** are commemorated during recitation of successive decades (sections of 10 beads) of prayer. (For more information about *How to Pray the Rosary,* see page 106.)

A MARRIAGE PROPOSAL

Pope Benedict XVI, speaking at World Youth Day in 2008, characterized God's covenant with Israel as a period of courtship, a long engagement followed by establishment of an everlasting covenant: "As Mary stood before the Lord, she represented the whole of humanity. In the angel's message, it was as if God made a marriage proposal to the human race. And in our name, Mary said yes." Mary's assent to God is repeated each time a Catholic responds by saying "Amen" when receiving the Eucharist, the sign of the New Covenant.

FRUITS OF PRAYER

HUMILITY

Each Mystery of the Rosary traditionally is associated with a particular fruit, or virtue. In addition to meditating on an individual Mystery, Christians can ask for an increase in the virtue tied to that Mystery.

The virtues associated with the Rosary are called fruits because they are the fruitful results of prayer. These virtues are planted as seeds during meditation, and understanding and practice of these virtues grow whenever Christians cultivate regular devotion to praying the Rosary.

When praying the first Joyful Mystery, the Annunciation, it has become traditional to ask for an increase in the virtue of humility. Just as the Blessed Virgin Mary humbly accepts her call from God to be the Mother of Jesus, Christians ask God for the grace to accept God's will for their lives.

Think about your life. What kind of action could God be calling you to right now that would further his kingdom? Will you say to God: "Let it be done to me according to your Word"?

Just as the Holy Spirit equipped Mary to become the Mother of the Savior, so also will God give you the power of the Holy Spirit to carry out any task to which he is calling you.

Hannah receives the promise of a son.

> **"** An understanding of transformative victory teaches us that it occurs in God's time, not ours, calling for our patient trust and deep hope in God. Hannah witnessed to such patient trust and hope. After many years of waiting to be pregnant, she prayed to God for a child, at the risk of having her weeping prayer dismissed as drunkenness by the priest at the doorpost of the Temple. When Eli assured her that God would grant her prayer, she simply trusted, waited, and was sad no longer. The great victory here is not that of nations or armies, but a glimpse into the realm of a private and personal struggle. In the end, Hannah's trust and hope results not only in her own transformation, but that of her people, for whom the God of Israel intervened through her son Samuel. **"**
>
> —2012 Pontifical Council for Promoting Christian Unity

1 SAMUEL 1:9–17

⁹After they had eaten and drunk in Shiloh, Hannah rose. Now Eli the priest was sitting on the seat beside the doorpost of the temple of the LORD. ¹⁰She was deeply distressed and prayed to the LORD, and wept bitterly. ¹¹And she vowed a vow and said, "O LORD of hosts, if you will indeed look on the affliction of your maidservant, and remember me, and not forget your maidservant, but will give to your maidservant a son, then I will give him to the LORD all the days of his life, and no razor shall touch his head."

¹²As she continued praying before the LORD, Eli observed her mouth. ¹³Hannah was speaking in her heart; only her lips moved, and her voice was not heard; therefore Eli took her to be a drunken woman. ¹⁴And Eli said to her, "How long will you be drunken? Put away your wine from you." ¹⁵But Hannah answered, "No, my lord, I am a woman sorely troubled; I have drunk neither wine nor strong drink, but I have been pouring out my soul before the LORD. ¹⁶Do not regard your maidservant as a base woman, for all along I have been speaking out of my great anxiety and vexation." ¹⁷Then Eli answered, "Go in peace, and the God of Israel grant your petition which you have made to him."

5 In *Luke* 1:34–35, what practical concern does the Blessed Virgin Mary raise when she learns that she is to become the mother of the Messiah? When the archangel Gabriel responds to Mary's concern, who does he tell her will be the father of her child?

6 Like many women in the Old Testament, Hannah is unable to conceive a child until God intervenes. Some of the most famous of these other women include Sarah (see *Genesis* 15:1—18:15), Rachel (see *Genesis* 29:9—30:24), and the wife of Manoah (see *Judges* 13:2–25). Compare each of their situations with Hannah's (see *1 Samuel* 1:1–8). Explain which of these four women you think exhibited the most faith-filled response to her barrenness. Explain which of these women's responses you think seems the most desperate.

7 What promise does Hannah make to God in her prayer (see *1 Samuel* 1:9–11)? Read about the Nazarites in *Numbers* 6:1–8. What does Hannah's promise suggest about the son she will bear?

8 What important lessons do you think contemporary Christians can learn about prayer from reading Hannah's story?

9 What mistake does the priest Eli make concerning Hannah's distraught condition (see *1 Samuel* 1:13–14)? Although Eli has not heard the specifics of Hannah's prayer, he adds his own prayer to hers. The Church fathers have seen in this a prophecy that God will grant Hannah's petition. What do you think prompts Eli to do this?

10 What is Hannah's response when the priest Eli tells her to go in peace (see *1 Samuel* 1:18)? What do you think that this suggests about Hannah's faith?

THE UNICORN AS A SYMBOL OF CHRIST

The unicorn, a mythical animal that appears at the top of the Annunciation Window (*page 22*), often is seen in medieval art as a symbol of Jesus Christ.

The unicorn usually is depicted in a forest scene paired with a young maiden, who represents the Blessed Virgin Mary. Legend held that the horn of the unicorn was capable of bringing about miraculous medical cures, which led to it becoming associated with Jesus as a symbol of salvation.

Although the King James Version, the Douay-Rheims, and some other translations of the Bible mention the unicorn in several passages (including *Numbers* 23:22; *Numbers* 24:8, *Job* 39:9–10, *Psalm* 92:10 [*Psalm* 92:11 NAB] and *Isaiah* 34:7), most modern translations substitute "wild ox."

A WOMAN SORELY TROUBLED

The Old Testament parallels to the Joyful Mysteries focus on the story of Hannah, a self-described "maidservant of the LORD." In the lower Annunciation Window, Hannah has been weeping and praying because she is unable to bear a child. The priest Eli mistakes her prayerful state for drunkenness. She denies this, and tells him of her distress. Eli then is inspired to add his own prayer to Hannah's, even though he is unaware of her barrenness.

Paragraph 489 of the *Catechism of the Catholic Church* teaches: "Throughout the Old Covenant the mission of many holy women *prepared* for that of Mary. At the very beginning there was Eve; despite her disobedience, she receives the promise of a posterity that will be victorious over the evil one.... Against all human expectation God chooses those who were considered powerless and weak to show forth his faithfulness to his promises."

It is significant that Hannah has promised to give her child back to God. The son to be born is Samuel, who is a transitional figure in the Old Testament, occupying a unique position as the last of the judges to step in to assist the people of Israel during times of trouble—and also as the first in a long line of prophets called to anoint and counsel the kings of Israel.

MARY AROSE AND WENT WITH HASTE

LUKE 1:39–57

[39]In those days Mary arose and went with haste into the hill country, to a city of Judah, [40]and she entered the house of Zechariah and greeted Elizabeth. [41]And when Elizabeth heard the greeting of Mary, the child leaped in her womb; and Elizabeth was filled with the Holy Spirit [42]and she exclaimed with a loud cry, "Blessed are you among women, and blessed is the fruit of your womb! [43]And why is this granted me, that the mother of my Lord should come to me? [44]For behold, when the voice of your greeting came to my ears, the child in my womb leaped for joy. [45]And blessed is she who believed that there would be a fulfilment of what was spoken to her from the Lord." [46]And Mary said,

"My soul magnifies the Lord,
[47]and my spirit rejoices in God my Savior,
[48]for he has regarded the low estate of his handmaiden.
For behold, henceforth all generations
 will call me blessed;
[49]for he who is mighty has done great things for me,
and holy is his name.
[50]And his mercy is on those who fear him
from generation to generation.
[51]He has shown strength with his arm,
he has scattered the proud in the imagination
 of their hearts,
[52]he has put down the mighty from their thrones,
and exalted those of low degree;
[53]he has filled the hungry with good things,
and the rich he has sent empty away.
[54]He has helped his servant Israel
in remembrance of his mercy,
[55]as he spoke to our fathers,
to Abraham and to his posterity for ever."

[56]And Mary remained with her about three months, and returned to her home.

[57]Now the time came for Elizabeth to be delivered, and she gave birth to a son.

The biblical text that describes the Blessed Virgin Mary's visit to the pregnant Elizabeth is the source of two Marian prayers.

A portion of Elizabeth's greeting to Mary has been incorporated into the Hail Mary, which is the primary prayer of the Rosary. And it is during Mary's visit to Elizabeth that the Blessed Virgin utters the prayer known as her Magnificat (*Luke* 1:46–55), a canticle that is prayed at Vespers each evening as part of Liturgy of the Hours.

How many other Marian prayers do you know? Which Marian prayer is your favorite, and what do you especially like about your choice?

What quality of the Blessed Virgin Mary do you find most attractive, and why? In what ways do you think that your life might change if you were to imitate Mary more closely?

1 Descriptions of people filled with the Holy Spirit occur almost exclusively in the New Testament. Most Old Testament figures are described as having the Spirit of God "come upon" them or be "in" them; they are not described as being "filled." Exceptions can be found in *Exodus* 31:1–5 and *Exodus* 35:30—36:1. In those passages, who does God fill with the Holy Spirit, and for what purpose?

2 In *Luke* 1:41, what is happening when Elizabeth becomes filled with the Holy Spirit? For what purpose do you think this occurs?

3 Paragraph 717 of the *Catechism of the Catholic Church* teaches that John the Baptist was "filled with the Holy Spirit even from his mother's womb." For what purpose do you think that John is filled with the Holy Spirit? Compare your answer with Church teaching found in paragraph 718 of the *Catechism of the Catholic Church*.

4 To be blessed can mean to be made holy or consecrated for a special purpose, to be endowed with divine favor and protection, or to be made happy. Which meaning or meanings do you think Elizabeth intends in *Luke* 1:42 and in *Luke* 1:45? Which meaning or meanings do you think that Mary intends in *Luke* 1:48? Which meaning or meanings do you think is indicated when the Church refers to the Mother of Jesus as "the Blessed Virgin Mary"?

5 Although Luke records only a small portion of conversation between the Blessed Virgin Mary and Elizabeth, the two women must have talked much more about God's love during the three months they were together. What do you usually talk about when you spend time with your relatives and closest friends? When was the last time that God's love and mercy were the topics of your everyday conversation? What great things has God done for you?

FRUITS OF PRAYER

LOVE OF NEIGHBOR

When asked "Teacher, which is the greatest commandment in the law?" Jesus sums up all the law and the prophets in two commandments: Love God completely, and "love your neighbor as yourself" (*Matthew* 22:36–40). Love of neighbor is a virtue that the Blessed Virgin Mary exemplifies in the second Joyful Mystery.

Rather than being self-absorbed in her own news, the young Virgin Mary, after learning that her relative Elizabeth is six months pregnant, immediately sets out to visit her. Mary stays for the final stages of Elizabeth's pregnancy before John the Baptist is born.

Jesus tells the parable of the Good Samaritan (*Luke* 10:25–37) in response to a lawyer who has asked what he must do to inherit eternal life. Upon learning that love of neighbor is involved, the lawyer asks Jesus: "And who is my neighbor?"

Think of people in your life whom you consider to be your neighbors. Who might you be leaving out? Identify one or two people who are undergoing special challenges. What are their needs? What are you doing to love and support them right now?

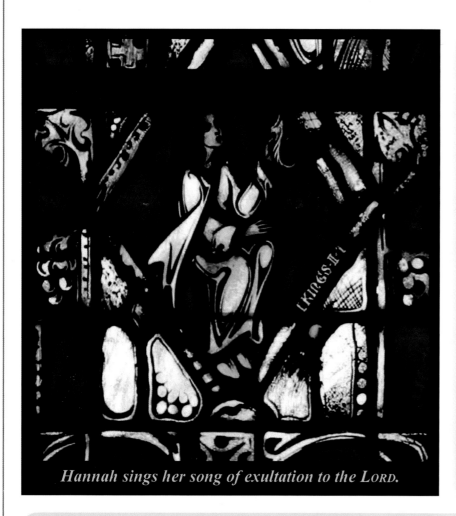

Hannah sings her song of exultation to the LORD.

HANNAH'S CANTICLE

The lower Visitation Window depicts Hannah as a young woman holding up a horn as she sings. *1 Samuel* 2:1 can be translated as "my horn is exalted," and the horn is seen as a symbol of strength. A comparison of Hannah's song and Mary's Magnificat shows many parallels. Both prayers acknowledge God's greatness, and both women express praise and thanksgiving. Both freely abandon themselves into the hands of Divine Providence.

Pope Benedict XVI, speaking at World Youth Day in 2008, taught that Mary's prayer goes beyond the surface: "Mary 'sees' with the eyes of faith God's work in history. For this reason she is blessed, because she believed." To a lesser extent, the same is true of Hannah.

1 SAMUEL 2:1–9

¹Hannah also prayed and said,
"My heart exults in the LORD;
   my strength is exalted in the LORD.
My mouth derides my enemies,
   because I rejoice in your salvation.
²There is none holy like the LORD,
   there is none besides you;
   there is no rock like our God.
³Talk no more so very proudly,
   let not arrogance come from your mouth;
for the LORD is a God of knowledge,
   and by him actions are weighed.
⁴The bows of the mighty are broken,
   but the feeble gird on strength.
⁵Those who were full have hired themselves
   out for bread,

but those who were hungry have ceased to
   hunger.
The barren has borne seven,
   but she who has many children is forlorn.
⁶The LORD kills and brings to life;
   he brings down to Sheol and raises up.
⁷The LORD makes poor and makes rich;
   he brings low, he also exalts.
⁸He raises up the poor from the dust;
   he lifts the needy from the dung heap,
to make them sit with princes
   and inherit a seat of honor.
For the pillars of the earth are the LORD's,
   and on them he has set the world.
⁹He will guard the feet of his faithful ones;
   but the wicked shall be cut off in darkness...."

6 Compare the Magnificat of the Blessed Virgin Mary (*Luke* 1:46–55) with the Canticle of Hannah (*1 Samuel* 2:1–8). How are the two canticles similar? In what ways do they differ? Which verses in Mary's Magnificat indicate her strong Jewish faith?

worldly–universal   personal

7 Explain which verses in Hannah's canticle might be interpreted as pointing ahead to the promise of a Messiah.

8 One verse in Hannah's canticle—"The LORD kills and brings to life" (*1 Samuel* 2:6)—emphasizes God's authority over life and death. How do you think that Hannah's life experiences may have contributed to her understanding (refer to *1 Samuel* 1:9–17 and *A Woman Sorely Troubled* on page 25)? What are some ways in which the modern world attempts to deny God's authority over life and death?

man after my own heart

9 At the top of the Visitation Window a flower symbolizes the blossoming of the stump of Jesse foretold in *Isaiah* 11:1, a prophecy that the Messiah would be born into the line of David, whose father was named Jesse. What quality did David possess that led to him being made "a prince over God's people" (see *1 Samuel* 13:14 and *Acts* 13:22)? If David is a prince, who do you think is the king? *Whole dear Jesus take place*

10 The word canticle originally meant a brief song. The word canticle now is used to refer to a liturgical hymn or chant based on a biblical text. The three most common New Testament canticles are found in *Luke's Gospel*—Mary's Magnificat (*Luke* 1:46–55), the Canticle of Zechariah (*Luke* 1:68–79), and the Canticle of Simeon (*Luke* 2:22–32). What overall theme do these three canticles have in common? Why do you think that Luke chose to feature these canticles in the introductory chapters of his Gospel?

Mag•nif•i•cat
a canticle of Mary prayed in Christian liturgy

In the opening verse from which the **Magnificat** takes its name, the Blessed Virgin Mary sings: "My soul magnifies the Lord" (*Luke* 1:46). To magnify means to make something appear larger. Paragraph 2675 of the *Catechism of the Catholic Church* explains that Marian prayers "magnify" the Lord for the "great things" he did for his lowly servant and through her for all human beings, while entrusting the supplications of the children of God to the Mother of Jesus, "because she now knows the humanity which, in her, the Son of God espoused." Praying the **Magnificat**, Christians consider the "great things" that God has done, and they join their prayer to Mary's in order that the Lord might be "magnified."

FILLED WITH THE HOLY SPIRIT

In the Visitation Window, a dove hovers overhead to indicate the presence of the Holy Spirit, and Scripture records that at the sound of Mary's voice Elizabeth is filled with the Holy Spirit. Elizabeth and John the Baptist in her womb are the first to recognize the arrival of the Savior in the world. This is a foreshadowing of the important role John the Baptist later will play as an adult when he announces the coming of the Messiah (*John* 1:19–29).

The visit of the Blessed Virgin Mary to Elizabeth points to God's willingness to take on human form in the Incarnation of Jesus Christ. Paragraph 717 of the *Catechism of the Catholic Church* teaches:

"John was 'filled with the Holy Spirit even from his mother's womb' by Christ himself, whom the Virgin Mary had just conceived by the Holy Spirit. Mary's visitation to Elizabeth thus became a visit from God to his people."

This idea also is expressed in the opening verse of the Canticle of Zechariah (*Luke* 1:68–79). The strange events surrounding the birth of John the Baptist lead his father to proclaim: "Blessed be the Lord God of Israel, for he has visited and redeemed his people." The Church traditionally prays Zechariah's canticle at Lauds (morning prayer) and Mary's Magnificat at Vespers (evening prayer).

A DECREE WENT OUT FROM CAESAR

Nov 15

The story of Jesus' birth comes to life in the Nativity Window, which provides a glimpse into the profound joy experienced by the Holy Family. Joy can be described as an emotion brought about by hearts overflowing with love.

In his midnight Mass for Christmas 2007, Pope Benedict XVI said that heaven is not so much a physical location but belongs to the "geography of the heart." This means that heaven is not a specific place but is instead a way of relating to God and others. The love that binds the Holy Family reflects the love that unites the persons of the Blessed Trinity.

Think of an occasion when your heart overflowed with joy and love. What brought about those emotions? What is a cause of joy in your life right now, and how can you share this joy with those who are closest to you?

LUKE 2:1–12

[1]In those days a decree went out from Caesar Augustus that all the world should be enrolled. [2]This was the first enrollment, when Quirinius was governor of Syria. [3]And all went to be enrolled, each to his own city. [4]And Joseph also went up from Galilee, from the city of Nazareth, to Judea, to the city of David, which is called Bethlehem, because he was of the house and lineage of David, [5]to be enrolled with Mary his betrothed, who was with child. [6]And while they were there, the time came for her to be delivered. [7]And she gave birth to her first-born son and wrapped him in swaddling cloths, and laid him in a manger, because there was no place for them in the inn.

[8]And in that region there were shepherds out in the field, keeping watch over their flock by night. [9]And an angel of the Lord appeared to them, and the glory of the Lord shone around them, and they were filled with fear. [10]And the angel said to them, "Be not afraid; for behold, I bring you good news of a great joy which will come to all the people; [11]for to you is born this day in the city of David a Savior, who is Christ the Lord. [12]And this will be a sign for you: you will find a baby wrapped in swaddling cloths and lying in a manger."

1 The Proclamation of the Birth of Christ, solemnly read in many Catholic churches at Christmas, dates Jesus' birth in relationship to other events in salvation history. It includes this line describing the condition of the world at the birth of the Messiah:

"The forty-second year of the reign of Octavian Augustus;
the whole world being at peace,
Jesus Christ, eternal God and Son of the eternal Father,
desiring to sanctify the world by his most merciful coming,
being conceived by the Holy Spirit,
and nine months having passed since his conception,
was born in Bethlehem of Judea of the Virgin Mary."

Compare this condition of the world at the time Jesus was born with the condition of the world at the time God promised to make David's kingdom last forever (see *2 Samuel* 7:1–2). In *2 Samuel* 5:1–5, David reunited the 12 tribes into one kingdom. What does this suggest about the relationship existing among the 12 tribes at that time?

2 Locate as many references to peace as you can in the messianic prophecies found in *Isaiah* 11:1–16. Against whom does Isaiah prophesy that the LORD will extend his hand, and for what purpose? When do you think that this prophecy will be fulfilled?

HEAVEN'S HARMONY

The mystery of the Incarnation is one of the key doctrines of the Christian faith. Animals in the stable witness Jesus' birth, and at the top of the Nativity Window the star of Bethlehem shines brightly on the scene. The message of Christmas makes men and women recognize the darkness of the closed world, yet the birth of Christ also demonstrates that God does not allow himself to be shut out and kept apart from his people. He finds a space, even if it means entering through a stable.

The light of Christmas shines forth from that stable for all time. "Whether we are shepherds or wise men, the light and its message call us to set out, to leave the narrow circle of our desires and interests, to go out to meet the Lord and worship him," Pope Benedict said in 2007 at his Christmas Midnight Mass. "We worship Jesus by opening the world to truth, to goodness, to Christ, and to the service of those who are marginalized and in whom he awaits us."

Jesus comes to restore beauty and dignity to all of Creation. It is for this reason that the angels rejoice at his birth. Harmony between human will and divine will is restored in the person of Jesus. It is the encounter with Jesus Christ that makes men and women capable of hearing the heavenly song of the angels—and once hearing the Good News, of sharing it with others.

FRUITS OF PRAYER

POVERTY OF SPIRIT

In his Sermon on the Mount, Jesus proclaims those who are "poor in spirit" to be blessed, and he promises that "theirs is the kingdom of heaven." This is the first of the eight beatitudes, or blessings, Jesus teaches in *Matthew* 5:1-12. Those who possess the virtue of poverty of spirit can see some blessing in every situation, and they accept all things as gifts from God.

Unable to find a room in the inn for Jesus' birth, Joseph still is able to find shelter. The third Joyful Mystery calls Christians to have the same attitude as the Blessed Virgin Mary and Joseph have regarding their earthly possessions and resources.

The issue addressed by this virtue is not so much a concern about what one has, but rather detachment from the things of the world. Christian desire seeks to accept all things with a thankful heart in order to share with others gifts given by God.

Think about your own material possessions. Ask God to help you take the necessary steps that will increase your poverty of spirit and will bless your life and the lives of others with corresponding spiritual richness.

Hannah keeps Samuel at home until he is weaned.

1 SAMUEL 1:19–23

¹⁹[Elkanah and Hannah] rose early in the morning and worshiped before the LORD; then they went back to their house at Ramah. And Elkanah knew Hannah his wife, and the LORD remembered her; ²⁰and in due time Hannah conceived and bore a son, and she called his name Samuel, for she said, "I have asked him of the LORD."

²¹And the man Elkanah and all his house went up to offer to the LORD the yearly sacrifice, and to pay his vow. ²²But Hannah did not go up, for she said to her husband, "As soon as the child is weaned, I will bring him, that he may appear in the presence of the LORD, and abide there for ever." ²³Elkanah her husband said to her, "Do what seems best to you, wait until you have weaned him; only, may the LORD establish his word." So the woman remained and nursed her son, until she weaned him.

THE BIRTH OF SAMUEL

The lower section of the Nativity Window depicts Hannah's joy at the birth of her son, Samuel. Samuel stands as one of the great transitional figures in the Old Testament. He is considered the last of the judges, those men and women who lead and direct the people of Israel in lieu of a king.

The Israelites, however, are not happy with this arrangement, which essentially amounts to having God as their king. They petition Samuel to allow them to have a human ruler—like other nations. Samuel attempts to dissuade them from this idea (*1 Samuel* 8:10–18), but they insist on an earthly king. Samuel's intimate relationship with God is apparent in *1 Samuel* 8:21–22: "And when Samuel had heard all the words of the people, he repeated them in the ears of the LORD. And the LORD said to Samuel, 'Listen to their voice, and make them a king.'"

Samuel does as he is told, anointing Saul and then David as king over the 12 tribes of Israel. Thus Samuel reluctantly becomes first in a long line of Old Testament prophets sent by God to counsel and guide the kings of Israel—and later the kings of Judah after the Davidic kingdom divides following the reign of Solomon.

The birth of Samuel ushers in a new era for God's chosen people, signaling a change in rulers. The birth of Jesus also ushers in a new era and a very different kind of kingdom.

3 Caesar Augustus was hailed in his time as "savior of the whole world" because he restored peace to the ancient world. In the Beatitudes, what promise does Jesus make to those who seek peace (see *Matthew* 5:9)? How can you find more peace in your life?

4 What does Jesus do that earns him the title "Prince of Peace" (see *CCC* 2305)? This title is found in an often-quoted Old Testament messianic prophecy of Isaiah. By what other titles is Jesus referred to in that prophecy (see *Isaiah* 9:6 [*Isaiah* 9:5 NAB])?

5 Jesus' earthly father is Joseph. What important inheritance does Jesus receive from Joseph (see *2 Samuel* 7:3–16)? In the *Letter to the Romans* 8:29, St. Paul describes Jesus as "the first-born among many brethren." Who are these brethren? Whose Son does St. Paul believe Jesus to be, and who is the Father of these many brethren?

6 In writing about the birth of Jesus, Luke mentions the census enrollment several times. Why do Mary and Joseph have to travel to Bethlehem to be enrolled? How does this fulfill an Old Testament prophecy of the prophet Micah (see *Micah* 5:2 [*Micah* 5:1 NAB])?

7 Although the occupation of shepherd lacks prestige, there were many shepherds favored by God in the Old Testament. Who are some of these famous shepherds, and in what ways were they blessed by God (see *Genesis* 4:2–4, *Genesis* 31:1–13, *Genesis* 37:2–11, *Exodus* 3:1–6, and *1 Samuel* 16:11–13)? Why do you think that God chose to reveal the birth of his Son to lowly shepherds? With which of these shepherds is Hannah's son Samuel connected?

8 In *John* 10:11, Jesus identifies himself as the Good Shepherd. What does Jesus say the Good Shepherd does for the sheep? According to Old Testament prophecy, why does the flock of Israel have need of a shepherd (see *Isaiah* 53:6)? Read *Psalm* 23. What are the advantages of belonging to the flock of the Divine Shepherd?

9 *Luke* 2:9 records that the glory of the Lord shone around the shepherds, and in *Luke* 2:14, the angel is joined by a multitude of the heavenly host praising God's glory. Paragraph 705 of the *Catechism of the Catholic Church* equates God's glory with the "likeness of the God." *John* 1:18 explains that God's likeness is made manifest in his Son, Jesus Christ. Describe how the Incarnation fulfills God's promises to the Old Testament patriarchs (see *CCC* 706).

10 Paragraph 705 of the *Catechism of the Catholic Church* also equates God's glory with the Holy Spirit, "the giver of life." How is the presence of the Holy Spirit at Creation related to the Holy Spirit's presence at the Incarnation? Explain the roles of the other two persons of the Blessed Trinity—God the Father and Jesus the Son—at Creation and at the Incarnation (see *John* 1:1–5)?

> **"** Where then is the dominion of the "Wonderful Counselor, Mighty God and Prince of Peace" of which the prophet Isaiah speaks? What is the power to which Jesus himself refers when he says: "All power has been given to me in heaven and on earth" (*Matthew* 28:18)? Christ's kingdom is "not of this world" (*John* 18:36).
>
> His kingdom is not the play of force and wealth and conquest that appear to shape our human history. It is rather the power to vanquish the Evil One, the ultimate victory over sin and death. It is the power to heal the wounds that disfigure the image of the Creator in his creatures. Christ's is the power to transform our weak nature and make us capable, through the grace of the Holy Spirit, of peace with one another and communion with God himself. "To all who received him, who believed in his name, he gave power to become children of God" (*John* 1:12).
>
> This is the message of Bethlehem today and for ever. This is the extraordinary gift that the Prince of Peace brought into the world two thousand years ago. Today from Manger Square, we cry out to every time and place, and to every person, "Peace be with you! Do not be afraid!" …They are the words of the Church to you today. Do not be afraid to preserve your Christian presence and heritage in the very place where the Savior was born. **"**
>
> —Blessed John Paul II
> 22 March 2000

A LIGHT FOR REVELATION TO THE GENTILES

The season of Christmas occurs at the darkest time of the year, something that serves to emphasize the miracle of the Incarnation. Think back to when you first began to grasp an understanding of Jesus as light of the world. In what practical ways can you help to spread the light of Christ now?

LUKE 2:22–35

22And when the time came for their purification according to the law of Moses, they brought him up to Jerusalem to present him to the Lord 23(as it is written in the law of the Lord, "Every male that opens the womb shall be called holy to the Lord") 24and to offer a sacrifice according to what is said in the law of the Lord, "a pair of turtledoves, or two young pigeons." 25Now there was a man in Jerusalem, whose name was Simeon, and this man was righteous and devout, looking for the consolation of Israel, and the Holy Spirit was upon him. 26And it had been revealed to him by the Holy Spirit that he should not see death before he had seen the Lord's Christ. 27And inspired by the Spirit he came into the temple; and when the parents brought in the child Jesus, to do for him according to the custom of the law, 28he took him up in his arms and blessed God and said,

29"Lord, now let your servant depart in peace, according to your word;

30for my eyes have seen your salvation

31which you have prepared in the presence of all peoples,

32a light for revelation to the Gentiles,

and for glory to your people Israel."

33And his father and his mother marveled at what was said about him; 34and Simeon blessed them and said to Mary his mother,

"Behold, this child is set for the fall and rising of many in Israel,

and for a sign that is spoken against

(and a sword will pierce through your own soul also),

35that thoughts out of many hearts may be revealed."

1 When Simeon thanks God for allowing him to see the Messiah, "a light for revelation to the Gentiles," he is borrowing from an Old Testament messianic prophecy: "The people who walked in darkness have seen a great light." Read *Isaiah* 9:1–7 (*Isaiah* 8:23–9:6 NAB). What is the nature of the darkness that has been plaguing the people?

2 *Isaiah* 9:6 (*Isaiah* 9:5 NAB) honors a royal child who's prophe-sied to become an ideal Davidic king and to reunite the 12 tribes of Israel. Compare language used by Isaiah to describe this child with language used in *Psalm* 45 to praise kings. What does Simeon's canticle (*Luke* 2:29–32) imply about the extent of the new kingdom?

3 What does the Isaian passage foretell about the nature and type of kingdom over which the Messiah will rule? How long will it last? How is this kingdom going to come into existence?

4 Simeon has been promised by God that he will not die before seeing the Messiah, and he blesses God when he sees the infant being presented at the Temple. How do you think that Simeon was made aware of God's promise that he would see the Messiah, and how do you think he knows that the infant Jesus is the Messiah?

THE SIGN OF THE COVENANT

Luke 2:21 records that Mary and Joseph had Jesus circumcised, a ritual established in the Old Testament as the sign of the covenant between God and Abraham (*Genesis* 17:9–14). God's promises to Abraham are great: "I will make you exceedingly fruitful; and I will make nations of you, and kings shall come forth from you. And I will establish my covenant between me and you and your descendants after you throughout their generations for an everlasting covenant, to be God to you and to your descendants after you" (*Genesis* 17:6–7). Abram has just been renamed Abraham (*Genesis* 17:5), and he also is promised the land of Canaan (*Genesis* 17:8).

Jesus' circumcision points to his fulfillment of all of God's prom-ises to the chosen people. Covenants involve both a sacrifice and a sign. The pair of turtledoves in the window represent the sacrifice of the Old Covenant (*Leviticus* 12:1–8); circumcision is its sign.

In the New Testament, Jesus institutes the sacrament of the Eucharist as the sign of the everlasting covenant: "And he took a chalice, and when he had given thanks he gave it to them, say-ing, 'Drink of it, all of you; for this is my blood of the covenant, which is poured out for many for the forgiveness of sins" (*Mat-thew* 26:27–28). This covenant is brought about through Jesus' sacrificial death. Baptism is the sign that replaces circumcision, the sign of the Old Covenant (*Colossians* 2:11–12).

OBEDIENCE

Obedience, the fruit of the fourth Joyful Mystery, is one of the most neglected virtues. Indeed, men and women seem determined to ignore obedience in favor of pursuing other paths to holiness.

Yet in *John* 14:15, Jesus teaches the importance of this virtue when he says: "If you love me, you will keep my commandments." He and the Blessed Virgin Mary both are obedient to God's commandments and to Jewish law.

The fourth Joyful Mystery of the Rosary not only calls Christians to obey God and his commandments, but to respect and obey all authority. Paragraph 1900 of the *Catechism of the Catholic Church* teaches: "The duty of obedience requires all to give due honor to authority and to treat those who are charged to exercise it with respect, and, insofar as it is deserved, with gratitude and good-will."

How seriously do you think that you take God's commandments? Who else is in authority over you at this point in your life? How do you think that you are doing at giving "due honor" and at showing respect, gratitude, and good will to your superiors?

Hannah dedicates her son to the Lord at Shiloh.

1 SAMUEL 1:24–28

²⁴And when [Hannah] had weaned [her son Samuel], she took him up with her, along with a three-year-old bull, an ephah of flour, and a skin of wine; and she brought him to the house of the Lord at Shiloh; and the child was young. ²⁵Then they slew the bull, and they brought the child to Eli. ²⁶And she said, "Oh, my lord! As you live, my lord, I am the woman who was standing here in your presence, praying to the Lord. ²⁷For this child I prayed; and the Lord has granted me my petition which I made to him. ²⁸Therefore I have lent him to the Lord; as long as he lives, he is lent to the Lord."

And they worshiped the Lord there.

SAMUEL OFFERED TO GOD

Hannah giving her son Samuel to the Lord parallels Jesus' presentation in the Temple. It is Jesus himself—Emmanuel, God-with-us (*Matthew* 1:23)— who is the dwelling of God, the true Temple. The devout Simeon is given the grace to recognize the infant Jesus as the long-awaited Messiah.

Simeon's Canticle (*Luke* 2:29–32) echoes Isaian prophecy read at Christmas: "The people who walked in darkness have seen a great light; those who dwelt in a land of deep darkness, on them has light shined. You have multiplied the nation, you have increased its joy; they rejoice before you as with joy at the harvest, as men rejoice when they divide the spoil.

"For the yoke of his burden, and the staff for his shoulder, the rod of his oppressor, you have broken as on the day of Midian….

"For to us a child is born, to us a son is given; and the government will be upon his shoulder, and his name will be called 'Wonderful Counselor, Mighty God, Everlasting Father, Prince of Peace.'

"Of the increase of his government and of peace there will be no end, upon the throne of David, and over his kingdom, to establish it, and to uphold it with justice and with righteousness from this time forth and for evermore. The zeal of the Lord of hosts will do this" (*Isaiah* 9:2–4, 6–7 [*Isaiah* 9:1–3, 5–6 NAB]).

5 What do you think that Simeon means in *Luke* 2:29 when he says: "Lord, now let your servant depart in peace"? Where is Simeon going, and why is he willing to depart now? What is the meaning of salvation, and how will it glorify God's people Israel?

6 How do the Blessed Virgin Mary and Joseph react when they hear Simeon praising God for the birth of Jesus? In *Luke* 2:34–35, what prophecies does Simeon make concerning Jesus? What well-known events that occur in Jesus' adult life can you see as fulfillment of Simeon's prophecies? How do you think that Jesus might continue to be a sign that is spoken against in the modern world?

7 In *Luke* 2:34–35, what does Simeon prophesy concerning the Blessed Virgin Mary? Paragraph 149 of the *Catechism of the Catholic Church* links this prophecy with Jesus' death on the cross. In what ways do you think that the two are related?

8 What is pierced at Jesus' Crucifixion (see *John* 19:31–37)? How does this piercing correspond to Old Testament prophecy found in *Zechariah* 12:10? According to *Zechariah* 13:1, what is the long-term significance of this for Jerusalem and for the house of David?

9 The Temple at the top of the Presentation Window is a reminder of God's dwelling with men and women. How does Baptism reflect Jewish purification rites (see *CCC* 2520)? As a sign of the New Covenant, Baptism replaces circumcision, the sign of the Old Covenant. Explain how Baptism changes the nature of the way that God dwells with humanity (see *CCC* 1265).

10 In *1 Samuel* 1:27–28, Hannah says that she has "lent" her son to the LORD. For how long a time does Hannah intend to lend her son to God? How is Hannah rewarded (see *1 Samuel* 2:18–21)? Compare Hannah's lending of Samuel to God with Abraham's willingness to sacrifice his son, Isaac (refer to *Genesis* 22:1–18 and *Isaac: The Heir of God's Promise* on page 16). Do you think one of these sacrifices is greater than the other? Explain your reasoning.

---

sal•va•tion deliverance from sin

The root of this word is the Greek *soteria*, which means safety. Although the word **salvation** frequently is used by Christians, Jesus uses it only twice in the Gospels (*Luke* 19:9 and *John* 4:22). The other four instances where **salvation** appears in the Gospels all occur in *Luke* (1:69, 1:77, 2:30, and 3:6). The first three are in the canticles, and the fourth occurs when John the Baptist quotes the Old Testament prophet Isaiah. In *Luke* 2:30, Simeon praises God for allowing him to see the newborn child who brings the opportunity of safety to all people of the world.

"This is the meeting point of the two Testaments, Old and New. The Child Jesus enters the ancient Temple; he who is the new Temple of God. He comes to visit his people, thus bringing to fulfillment obedience to the Law, and ushering in the last times of salvation.

It is interesting to take a close look at this entrance of the Child Jesus into the solemnity of the Temple, in the great comings and goings of many people, busy with their work: priests and Levites taking turns to be on duty, the numerous devout people and pilgrims anxious to encounter the Holy God of Israel. Yet none of them noticed anything. Jesus was a child like the others, a first-born son of very simple parents.

Even the priests proved incapable of recognizing the signs of the new and special presence of the Messiah and Savior. Alone two elderly people, Simeon and Anna, discover this great newness. Led by the Holy Spirit, in this Child they find the fulfillment of their long waiting and watchfulness. They both contemplate the light of God that comes to illuminate the world, and their prophetic gaze is opened to the future in the proclamation of the Messiah: *"Lumen ad revelationem gentium!"* (*Luke* 2:32). The prophetic attitude of the two elderly people contains the entire Old Covenant, which expresses the joy of the encounter with the Redeemer."

—Pope Benedict XVI
2 February 2011

ALL WHO HEARD HIM WERE AMAZED

The upper window representing the fifth Joyful Mystery of the Rosary depicts the boy Jesus in the Temple. His raised and pointed finger denotes teaching authority, and learned rabbis sit with their scrolls unfurled at his feet.

Paragraph 534 of the *Catechism of the Catholic Church* explains that in this event "Jesus lets us catch a glimpse of the mystery of his total consecration to a mission that flows from his divine sonship: 'Did you not know that I must be about my Father's work?' Mary and Joseph did not understand these words, but they accepted them in faith."

Think about words of Jesus that are difficult to understand. Ask Jesus to help you to accept these Christian mysteries with faith similar to that demonstrated by the Blessed Virgin Mary.

LUKE 2:41–52

[41]Now his parents went to Jerusalem every year at the feast of the Passover. [42]And when he was twelve years old, they went up according to custom; [43]and when the feast was ended, as they were returning, the boy Jesus stayed behind in Jerusalem. His parents did not know it, [44]but supposing him to be in the company they went a day's journey, and they sought him among their kinsfolk and acquaintances; [45]and when they did not find him, they returned to Jerusalem, seeking him. [46]After three days they found him in the temple, sitting among the teachers, listening to them and asking them questions; [47]and all who heard him were amazed at his understanding and his answers. [48]And when they saw him they were astonished; and his mother said to him, "Son, why have you treated us so? Behold, your father and I have been looking for you anxiously." [49]And he said to them, "How is it that you sought me? Did you not know that I must be in my Father's house?" [50]And they did not understand the saying which he spoke to them. [51]And he went down with them and came to Nazareth, and was obedient to them; and his mother kept all these things in her heart.

[52]And Jesus increased in wisdom and in stature, and in favor with God and man.

1 The hidden years of Jesus's life hold special fascination for Christians, yet the only Gospel mention of Jesus' childhood is found in *Luke* 2:41–52, the account of his parents finding him in the Temple. Paragraph 517 of the *Catechism of the Catholic Church* teaches: "Christ's whole life is a mystery of *redemption.* Redemption comes to us above all through the blood of his cross, but this mystery is at work throughout Christ's entire life." The *Catechism* goes on to explain that in Jesus' hidden life redemption can be seen in Jesus' submission. In what ways does the boy Jesus demonstrate a submissive nature? What is redemption (refer to *God's Only Son: Redemption & Hope* on pages 14–17)? How is Jesus' submission to his earthly parents connected with the redemption of humanity (refer to *CCC* 517)?

2 What does Scripture disclose about how often Jesus' family visited Jerusalem, and for what purpose? How old is Jesus when he stays behind his family to spend more time in the Temple? What religious feast is taking place in Jerusalem at the time that Jesus decides to stay behind? How do you think that this particular religious feast might relate to Jesus' mission of redemption?

3 How long do Jesus' earthly parents have to search before they locate him in the Temple in Jerusalem? What future event in Jesus' life do you think that this might foreshadow? What is Jesus doing when his parents find him? *Luke* 2:47 goes on to recount that all who heard Jesus were amazed at his understanding and his answers. What does this verse suggest that is not mentioned in *Luke* 2:46?

4 What things does *Luke* 2:52 imply result from Jesus' being obedient to his earthly parents? At what age do you think that it no longer is important for children to obey their parents? Which of the commandments given by God to the Israelites at Mt. Sinai is Jesus following by being obedient to Mary and Joseph (see *Exodus* 20:1–17)?

5 What emotions does the Blessed Virgin express in *Luke* 2:48? What else might Mary have been feeling when she learned that Jesus was missing? Why do you think that Jesus' earthly parents are unable to understand when he tells them that the Temple is his Father's house? What is Mary's ultimate response to these events?

THE INNER LIGHT OF FAITH

A hanging lamp burns brightly at the top of this window. A similar lamp appears in the primary scene depicted in the Presentation Window. In religious art, a lamp symbolizes the inner light of faith. In both windows it emphasizes Jesus' role as light of the nations, the Messiah who will bring revelation to all peoples. In Catholic churches, lighted sanctuary lamps are placed near the Tabernacle where the Eucharist reposes, and thus a lighted lamp in religious artwork also symbolizes the presence of Jesus.

FRUITS OF PRAYER

ZEAL FOR GOD
Zeal is the fruit of the fifth Joyful Mystery. Piety also occasionally is listed as a fruit of praying this Mystery.

The two virtues are closely related. True piety only can occur when one has zeal for God. Just as the young Jesus feels that he "must be" in his Father's house, Christians are called to be enthusiastic disciples, working tirelessly and diligently to further God's kingdom.

Do you find yourself absorbed in Scripture, hungry to learn more and to grow in virtue? Do you get lost in prayer, or spend time in conversations with others about your faith? What are the gifts that God has given you to help others? How much thought, time, and effort are you devoting to using these gifts in ministry? Were you once enthusiastic for things of God but now have found your interest has waned?

In the book of *Revelation*, Jesus warns early Christians at the Church in Laodicea against the danger of losing their zeal: "Would that you were cold or hot! So because you are lukewarm, and neither cold nor hot, I will spew you out of my mouth" (*Revelation* 3:15–16). What can you do to turn up the heat of the fire of your faith and Catholic practice?

Eli encourages Samuel to respond to God's call.

THE LORD CALLS SAMUEL

Obedience and listening figure prominently in the Old Testament parallel to Jesus' parents finding him in the Temple. The lower window shows the boy Samuel being called by God. The priest Eli, charged with Samuel's care, at first fails to grasp the significance of what is happening.

Once Eli recognizes that the LORD is calling Samuel, he advises the boy to return to where he has been resting. If the LORD calls again, Eli instructs Samuel, he is to tell God that he's prepared to listen, using these words: "Speak, LORD, for your servant hears."

Scripture emphasizes that visions were rare at the time when the LORD called Samuel. It is of note that the boy had been helping to minister in the Temple and was at rest near the ark of the covenant.

1 SAMUEL 3:1–9

¹Now the boy Samuel was ministering to the LORD under Eli. And the word of the LORD was rare in those days; there was no frequent vision. ²At that time Eli, whose eyesight had begun to grow dim, so that he could not see, was lying down in his own place; ³the lamp of God had not yet gone out, and Samuel was lying down within the temple of the LORD, where the ark of God was. ⁴Then the LORD called, "Samuel, Samuel!" and he said, "Here I am!" ⁵and ran to Eli, and said, "Here I am, for you called me." But he said, "I did not call; lie down again." So he went and lay down. ⁶And the LORD called again, "Samuel!" And Samuel arose and went to Eli and said, "Here I am, for you called me." But he said, "I did not call, my son; lie down again." ⁷Now Samuel did not yet know the LORD, and the word of the LORD had not yet been revealed to him. ⁸And the LORD called Samuel again the third time. And he arose and went to Eli, and said, "Here I am, for you called me." Then Eli perceived that the LORD was calling the boy. ⁹Therefore Eli said to Samuel, "Go, lie down; and if he calls you, you shall say, 'Speak, LORD, for your servant hears.'" So Samuel went and lay down in his place.

6 What role does the Temple at Jerusalem play in the fourth and the fifth Joyful Mysteries? In what ways do you think that the Temple is connected with joy? The Old Testament contains many examples of joy in connection with worship, including a number of the *Psalms* attributed to David. What key event in the life of David exemplifies his great joy in worshiping God (see *2 Samuel* 6:1–23)?

7 The Old Testament parallel to the fifth Joyful Mystery is the call of Samuel. Where is Samuel when God calls to him? According to the priest Eli, how should one correctly respond to God's call?

8 How does Samuel respond the fourth time that God calls, and what does the Lord tell Samuel (see *1 Samuel* 3:10–14)? How does Samuel feel about repeating what the Lord has told him (see *1 Samuel* 3:15)? What does Eli advise Samuel to do, and what is Eli's response when he learns what God has told Samuel (see *1 Samuel* 3:16–18)? Is Eli's response one that you would expect? What does Eli's response tell you about his faith and his character?

9 Read *1 Samuel* 8:4–22. How does Samuel feel about the Israelites' desire to be ruled by an earthly king? Who has been ruling the Israelites up until this time? What does Samuel warn will happen if the people insist on being ruled by an earthly king?

10 What does Saul do that causes him to fall out of favor with God (see *1 Samuel* 13:1–14)? What does Samuel prophesy will happen to Saul's kingdom? Samuel says that Saul is to be replaced as king by a man after God's own heart. Who does Samuel anoint as king of Israel after Saul (*1 Samuel* 16:1–13). In what ways do you think that this king foreshadows the reign of Jesus Christ?

A GREAT JUDGE & PROPHET

As the last of the Old Testament judges, Samuel advises the people against rejecting God as their ruler (*1 Samuel* 8:4–22), yet he follows God's command and anoints Saul as the first king over Israel (*1 Samuel* 9:27—10:7). Samuel is the first prophet in a line of many called to counsel the kings who rule over God's chosen people. When Saul refuses to follow God's commands, Samuel secretly anoints David as king (*1 Samuel* 16:1–13).

As a man after God's own heart, David is a type of Jesus. It is significant that David goes on to unite all 12 tribes of Israel (*2 Samuel* 5:1–5), and that Old Testament prophets foretell of a descendant of the house of David who will arise as Messiah to reunite the 12 tribes. Jesus does even more to fulfill messianic prophecy, expanding his eternal kingdom to include all people.

❝ The Evangelist Luke describes the young Jesus' pilgrimage to the Temple in Jerusalem as the last episode of the infancy narrative before the start of John the Baptist's preaching. It is an ordinary occasion that sheds light on the long years of his hidden life in Nazareth.

On this occasion, with his strong personality Jesus reveals that he is aware of his mission, giving to this second "entry" into his "Father's house" the meaning of his total gift of self to God, which already had marked his presentation in the Temple.

This passage seems to contrast with Luke's note that Jesus was obedient to Joseph and Mary. If one looks closely, here Jesus seems to put himself in a conscious and almost deliberate antithesis to his normal state as Son, unexpectedly causing a definite separation from Mary and Joseph....

Through this episode, Jesus prepares his Mother for the mystery of the Redemption. During those three dramatic days when the Son withdraws from them to stay in the Temple, Mary and Joseph experience an anticipation of the Triduum of his Passion, death, and Resurrection. Jesus brings them into the mystery of that suffering which leads to joy, anticipating what he would later accomplish with his disciples through the announcement of his Passover. ❞

—Blessed John Paul II
15 January 1997

HE BEGAN TO BE SORROWFUL

I n the window representing the first Sorrowful Mystery of the Rosary, Jesus is shown praying: "My Father, if it be possible, let this chalice pass from me; nevertheless, not as I will, but as you will" (*Matthew* 26:39).

The figures of Peter, James, and John appear dozing at the bottom of the scene, having been overcome by their human desire to sleep. Jesus' statement to them—"So you could not watch with me one hour?" (*Matthew* 26:40)—is an admonition that over the centuries has saddened many Christians who have nodded off while intending to pray.

Identify an area of your life that seems beyond your control. Set aside one hour this week to spend in uninterrupted prayer asking for the grace to accept whatever God wills.

MATTHEW 26:36–46

36Then Jesus went with them to a place called Gethsemane, and he said to his disciples, "Sit here, while I go over there and pray." 37And taking with him Peter and the two sons of Zebedee, he began to be sorrowful and troubled. 38Then he said to them, "My soul is very sorrowful, even to death; remain here, and watch with me." 39And going a little farther he fell on his face and prayed, "My Father, if it be possible, let this chalice pass from me; nevertheless, not as I will, but as you will." 40And he came to the disciples and found them sleeping; and he said to Peter, "So you could not watch with me one hour? 41Watch and pray that you may not enter into temptation; the spirit indeed is willing, but the flesh is weak." 42Again, for the second time, he went away and prayed, "My Father, if this cannot pass unless I drink it, your will be done." 43And again he came and found them sleeping, for their eyes were heavy. 44So, leaving them again, he went away and prayed for the third time, saying the same words. 45Then he came to the disciples and said to them, "Are you still sleeping and taking your rest? Behold, the hour is at hand, and the Son of man is betrayed into the hands of sinners. 46Rise, let us be going; see, my betrayer is at hand."

1 Jesus' agony in the Garden of Gethsemane can be understood as an occasion in which he is struggling and suffering with another contender in connection with some sort of a contest. Against whom do you think that Jesus is competing? Explain whether you think that the primary nature of this contest is physical, mental, emotional, or spiritual. What is the prize?

2 *Matthew* 14:22–23 records an instance in which Jesus went off by himself to pray. Why do you think that he asked three of his disciples to accompany him in the Garden of Gethsemane? In *Matthew* 26:37–38, who are the three disciples, and what specifically does Jesus ask them to do?

3 A common misunderstanding concerning Jesus' agony in the garden is that because Jesus is God, he had no choice about whether he would accept the chalice from his Father—in which case Jesus' anguished prayer in *Matthew* 26:39 would be a mere formality. How might this sort of thinking be dangerous to Christian faith? Explain how Church teaching addresses the issue (see *CCC* 475).

4 How do the disciples respond to Jesus' request that they watch with him? In *Matthew* 26:41, Jesus attributes their failure to do so to weakness of the flesh overcoming their willingness of spirit. Paragraph 2733 of the *Catechism of the Catholic Church* teaches that acedia is a form of spiritual depression due to "lax ascetical practice, decreasing vigilance, and carelessness of heart." According to St. Paul, what help is available for Christians seeking to overcome weakness of the flesh (*Romans* 8:26–27)?

5 In *Matthew* 26:45, when Jesus awakens his disciples, he tells them that "the hour is at hand." Read *John* 12:23–27. How is Jesus' emotional state in this passage similar to that described in *Matthew* 26:36–46? What additional light does the passage in *John* shed on the meaning of Jesus' "hour." Do you think that the disciples understand the seriousness of what is about to happen to Jesus?

---

ag•o•ny
extreme physical or mental suffering

The root of **agony** is the Greek *agonia*, which is related to a physical contest. While **agony** once was used only to describe physical suffering, in has come to include the meaning of mental and emotional suffering as well. The scene in the Garden of Gethsemane indeed represents a type of contest between Jesus' divine and human natures. That Jesus is in **agony** over the ordeal to come is obvious when he asks God to let the chalice of suffering pass. Jesus' divine nature is of course victorious, but his human suffering remains very real.

FRUITS OF PRAYER

SORROW FOR SIN

Sorrow for sin, or contrition, is the fruit associated with the first Sorrowful Mystery. Another fruit associated with this Mystery is conformity to the Word of God. Christians appropriately feel sorrow for sin while meditating on Jesus' Agony the Garden, since that is where Jesus experiences such sorrow for the sins of humanity.

It is hard for men and women to contemplate the face of pure Love and Truth and not draw back in shame. Christians find themselves identifying with Peter's great statement of contrition: "Depart from me, for I am a sinful man, O Lord" (*Luke* 5:8).

Followers of Jesus need to make a regular effort to look deep within their hearts and to repent of any evil thoughts, words, and actions that contribute to Jesus' agony and cause him to sweat blood in the Garden of Gethsemane.

After Peter faces his denials of Jesus, Scripture records that "he wept bitterly" (*Matthew* 26:75). In facing sin, men and women are grieved at having caused Jesus to suffer such torment. Resolve to seek the sacrament of Reconciliation in order to express sorrow for sin and seek God's forgiveness.

David, forced to leave Jerusalem, crosses the Kidron.

DAVID FLEES FROM JERUSALEM

In this Old Testament parallel to the first Sorrowful Mystery, David has been forced to leave Jerusalem because of an uprising led by his son.

David's upright nature is apparent as he tries to spare Ittai the Gittite the travail of fleeing the city, but Ittai insists on accompanying the king.

Scripture records that all the people weep as David crosses the Kidron. The valley of the Kidron is located between Jerusalem and the Garden of Gethsemane, which is at the foot of the Mount of Olives.

Jesus' Passion, which will bring about the redemption of all humanity, begins in a garden. This event is foreshadowed in the Garden of Eden, the site where the Fall took place (*Genesis* 3:1–24).

2 SAMUEL 15:13–16, 19–23

[13]And a messenger came to David, saying, "The hearts of the men of Israel have gone after Absalom." [14]Then David said to all his servants who were with him at Jerusalem, "Arise, and let us flee; or else there will be no escape for us from Absalom; go in haste, lest he overtake us quickly, and bring down evil upon us, and strike the city with the edge of the sword." [15]And the king's servants said to the king, "Behold, your servants are ready to do whatever my lord the king decides." [16]So the king went forth, and all his household after him ....

[19]Then the king said to Ittai the Gittite, "Why do you also go with us? Go back, and stay with the king; for you are a foreigner, and also an exile from your home. [20]You came only yesterday, and shall I today make you wander about with us, seeing I go I know not where? Go back, and take your brethren with you; and may the LORD show mercy and faithfulness to you." [21]But Ittai answered the king, "As the LORD lives, and as my lord the king lives, wherever my lord the king shall be, whether for death or for life, there also will your servant be." [22]And David said to Ittai, "Go then, pass on." So Ittai the Gittite passed on, with all his men and all the little ones who were with him. [23]And all the country wept aloud as all the people passed by, and the king crossed the brook Kidron, and all the people passed on toward the wilderness.

6 Read *2 Samuel* 13:1–39. What has caused the rift between King David and his son Absalom? According to *2 Samuel* 13:39, how does David feel about Absalom? How does this demonstrate that David is a man after God's own heart (see *1 Samuel* 13:14)?

7 Read *2 Samuel* 14:1–33. What happens to persuade David to allow Absalom to return to Jerusalem? What restrictions does the king place on Absalom living there? How long does Absalom live under those restrictions? How are the restrictions lifted?

8 Absalom's plot to win control of the kingdom is described in *2 Samuel* 15:1–12. Which role of King David does Absalom call into question? How long does Absalom engage in preparations to usurp his father's throne? What does Absalom say is the reason he wants permission to travel to Hebron? What is Absalom's real goal?

9 In *2 Samuel* 15:13-14, David learns of the conspiracy against him from a messenger. What does the king's response indicate concerning his feelings about fighting against his son? Explain whether you think that David is more concerned about the tragedy of his political situation or the tragedy within his family.

10 How does David's interest in the welfare of Ittai the Gittite in *2 Samuel* 15:19–23 demonstrate that David is a man after God's own heart? What else does it show about the sort of man that David is? What does Ittai's reaction indicate about his own character? How do you think that David's situation as he is fleeing from Jerusalem resembles Jesus' agony in the Garden of Gethsemane?

A MAN AFTER GOD'S OWN HEART

The lower windows showing Old Testament parallels to the Sorrowful Mysteries of the Rosary are based on tragic events in the life of David, a powerful Old Testament type of Jesus Christ. When Saul must be replaced as king, the prophet Samuel says of David: "the LORD has sought out a man after his own heart; and the LORD has appointed him to be prince over his people" (*1 Samuel* 13:14).

Despite his great love for God, details of David's life recorded in *1 and 2 Samuel* indicate that it was no bed of roses. The jealous Saul repeatedly attempts to kill David, yet David mourns Saul's death. David's wife, Saul's daughter, is unable to understand her husband's devotion to God. David himself piles sin upon sin when he commits adultery with Bathsheba and then conspires to have her husband killed. Finally, David's own son Absalom takes up arms against his father, forcing David to flee Jerusalem for his life.

After the invitation to stay with him to watch and pray, which he addresses to the three, Jesus speaks to the Father "alone." Mark the Evangelist tells us that "going a little farther, he fell on the ground and prayed that, if it were possible, the hour might pass from him" (*Mark* 14:35).

Jesus fell prostrate on the ground: a position of prayer that expresses obedience to the Father and abandonment in him with complete trust. This gesture is repeated at the beginning of the celebration of the Passion on Good Friday, as well as in monastic profession and in the ordination of deacons, priests, and bishops, in order to express, in prayer, corporally too, complete entrustment to God and trust in him. Jesus then asks the Father—if this be possible—to obtain that this hour pass from him. It is not only man's fear and anguish in the face of death, but is the devastation of the Son of God who perceives the terrible mass of evil that he must take upon himself to overcome it and to deprive it of power.

Dear friends, in prayer we too should be able to lay before God our labors, the suffering of certain situations, of certain days, the daily commitment to following him, to being Christian, and also the weight of the evil that we see within ourselves and around us, so that he may give us hope and make us feel his closeness and give us a little light on the path of life. **"**

—Pope Benedict XVI
1 February 2012

PILATE TOOK JESUS AND SCOURGED HIM

The window depicting the second Sorrowful Mystery of the Rosary focuses on Jesus' Scourging at the Pillar, a particularly unsettling event in Jesus' Passion. Though Jesus' scourging is horrifying, it highlights the ability of some members of humanity to engage in unthinkable cruelty.

No one in his right mind knowingly would torture God. Even taking into account God's unlimited capacity for forgiveness, who would want to accept responsibility for scourging God? The psychological effects alone would be debilitating.

Love is the reason that Jesus willingly suffered in order to redeem the sins of all of humanity. Love is the same reason that God forgives all of our sins, no matter how grave. Set aside some time during the next two weeks to thoroughly examine your conscience and to receive the sacrament of Reconciliation.

JOHN 18:33–19:1

[33]Pilate entered the praetorium again and called Jesus, and said to him, "Are you the King of the Jews?" [34]Jesus answered, "Do you say this of your own accord, or did others say it to you about me?" [35]Pilate answered, "Am I a Jew? Your own nation and the chief priests have handed you over to me; what have you done?" [36]Jesus answered, "My kingship is not of this world; if my kingship were of this world, my servants would fight, that I might not be handed over to the Jews; but my kingship is not from the world." [37]Pilate said to him, "So you are a king?" Jesus answered, "You say that I am a king. For this I was born, and for this I have come into the world, to bear witness to the truth. Every one who is of the truth hears my voice." [38]Pilate said to him, "What is truth?"

After he had said this, he went out to the Jews again, and told them, "I find no crime in him. [39]But you have a custom that I should release one man for you at the Passover; will you have me release for you the King of the Jews?" [40]They cried out again, "Not this man, but Barabbas!" Now Barabbas was a robber.

[1]Then Pilate took Jesus and scourged him.

truth love

1 In the eighteenth chapter of *John's Gospel*, Pontius Pilate tries to learn whether Jesus is King of the Jews. What do you think has prompted Pilate to ask this question? Explain how Pilate's behavior might change if Jesus were the ruler of a kingdom of "this world."

intrinsic given by God surrender

2 In *John* 18:36, Jesus says that if his kingship were of this world his servants would fight to prevent him being handed over to the Jews. What does this statement tell Pilate about Jesus' relationship with the Jews? Who do you think Jesus' servants are? What evidence is there that all of them might not understand that Jesus is not expecting them to fight (see *John* 18:10–11)? What does Jesus say to discourage his followers from violent behavior (see *Matthew* 26:52)?

Peter - Sword perish by holy spirit

3 What do you think that Jesus means when he tells Pilate: "For this I was born, and for this I have come into the world, to bear witness to the truth" (*John* 18:37)? According to paragraph 1954 of the *Catechism of the Catholic Church*, what is the relationship between truth and natural moral law? What do you think are the primary falsehoods challenging truth today in the contemporary world?

love one another as I have loved you

4 *Isaiah* 53:5 foretells Jesus' scourging in a prophecy about a suffering servant who would be "wounded for our transgressions" and "bruised for our iniquities." How did Peter come to view Jesus' suffering in relationship to Isaiah's prophecy (see *1 Peter* 2:24)?

because in God's plan

5 When Pilate offers to release Jesus for the Passover, the crowd demands Barabbas instead. What do you think Pilate's motivation is for having Jesus scourged (see *Luke* 23:13–22)? How does Pilate react when that fails to satisfy the crowd (see *Matthew* 27:24)?

WHAT IS TRUTH?

Pilate's primary misunderstanding in his dealings with Jesus is that Jesus does not simply admire and champion the truth, Jesus is Truth itself. Although it seems that it should be an easy matter to accept that God and Truth are synonymous, in the contemporary world many people show by the testimony of their lives that they do not hold the truth to be important. Considerations such as prestige, money, and power often take precedence.

Pilate's unwillingness to crucify an innocent man is overcome by other factors, which he undoubtedly finds compelling. In the account of Jesus' Passion in *John's Gospel*, the Roman procurator tries to rationalize his actions and the resulting cruelty by suggesting that objective truth does not exist. His thinking reflects the common idea that if there is no objective truth, then truth cannot be used as a standard by which to measure behavior.

MORAL PURITY

The cruel lashing of Jesus' innocent human flesh reminds Christians to honor their Savior's sacrifice by treating their own bodies with respect and dignity. The virtue associated with the second Sorrowful Mystery, the Scourging at the Pillar, is moral purity.

Moral purity also requires that men and women respect the bodies of others. Contemplating the scourging of Jesus, men and women are confronted with the price that Jesus paid in his own body. Throughout the history of the Church, Christians have sought to tame their flesh by mortifications such as wearing uncomfortable clothing or articles that scratched the skin as reminders of bodily purity.

Mortification takes place through spiritual disciplines and practices such as fasting and denying our whims and appetites. Wearing a wool scapular or a crucifix encourages moral purity, as do performing public displays of faith such as praying in restaurants and refusing to patronize businesses and establishments where the body is not respected.

Ask God to grant you an increase in moral purity and renewed respect for the dignity of the human body.

Shimei, a Benjaminite, casts stones at David.

SHIMEI CURSES DAVID

The Old Testament parallel to the second Sorrowful Mystery of the Rosary shows David being battered by stones as he flees Jerusalem to escape from Absalom. The man abusing David in this way is Shimei, a Benjaminite and a relative of Saul, who was displaced as king by David.

Scripture provides a glimpse into David's character when it records his response to one of his men's suggestion that Shimei be beheaded for bad behavior. Instead, David orders that Shimei be allowed to continue throwing stones: "Let him alone, and let him curse; for the LORD has bidden him. It may be that the LORD will look upon my affliction, and that the LORD will repay me with good for this cursing of me today!" (*2 Samuel* 16:12).

2 SAMUEL 16:5–12

⁵When King David came to Bahurim, there came out a man of the family of the house of Saul, whose name was Shimei, the son of Gera, and as he came he cursed continually. ⁶And he threw stones at David, and at all the servants of King David; and all the people and all the mighty men were on his right hand and on his left. ⁷And Shimei said as he cursed, "Begone, begone, you man of blood, you worthless fellow! ⁸The LORD has avenged upon you all the blood of the house of Saul, in whose place you have reigned; and the LORD has given the kingdom into the hand of your son Absalom. See, your ruin is on you, for you are a man of blood."

⁹Then Abishai the son of Zeruiah said to the king, "Why should this dead dog curse my lord the king? Let me go over and take off his head." ¹⁰But the king said, "What have I to do with you, you sons of Zeruiah? If he is cursing because the LORD has said to him, 'Curse David,' who then shall say, 'Why have you done so?'" ¹¹And David said to Abishai and to all his servants, "Behold, my own son seeks my life; how much more now may this Benjaminite! Let him alone, and let him curse; for the LORD has bidden him. ¹²It may be that the LORD will look upon my affliction, and that the LORD will repay me with good for this cursing of me today!"

6 In *2 Samuel* 16:5–12, the man who begins cursing David is described as a relative of Saul, a member of the tribe of Benjamin. What reason would one of Saul's relatives have for being so hostile toward David (see *1 Samuel* 16:1–13)? Explain whether you think that Shimei is justified in feeling resentment toward King David.

7 Although Shimei accuses David of being "a man of blood," Scripture indicates that David was pursued and persecuted by Saul, not the other way around. Read *2 Samuel* 1:1–16. What emotions does David express when he learns of Saul's death? David then has the messenger slain who brought him news of the death of Saul and Jonathan. What reason does David give for this? Do you think David's reason for having the messenger killed is valid?

8 What characteristics are shared by Abishai in *2 Samuel* 16:9 and Peter in *John* 18:10? How is David's response to Abishai's suggestion similar to Jesus' response to Peter's action?

9 In the Old Testament description of God's *suffering servant* suffering servant found in *Isaiah* 53:1–12, what ultimately happens to the servant? David's words in *2 Samuel* 16:10–12 reflect his hope that a similar fate may await him. What evidence is there to indicate that David is not presuming upon God's goodness?

10 Why do you think that Isaiah's portrait of the "man of sorrows" is the Old Testament reading chosen for Good Friday (see *Isaiah* 53:1–12)? In his silence before his accusers, Jesus fulfills the prophecy of *Isaiah* 53:7. Explain whether you think speaking out against unjust accusations necessarily is wrong.

MEN OF SORROWS

Isaiah 53:1–12 comprises the prophet's description of God's suffering servant. This Old Testament passage is a striking prophetic foreshadowing of the Passion of Jesus, and it is read as part of the Church's Good Friday liturgy.

Although David is credited with uniting the 12 tribes of Israel under one kingdom, his life includes tragedy and enough such incidents as that recorded in *2 Samuel* 16:5–12 that he also can be viewed as "a man of sorrows," "acquainted with grief," and one "despised and rejected of men" (*Isaiah* 53:3).

Interestingly, Isaiah's description of God's suffering servant points to another key link between David and Jesus—that of the reward promised to the righteous who bear iniquities and endure suffering. Although David follows Saul in the succession of rulers over the kingdom of Israel, it is not David's doing that causes Saul to lose the throne. David's acceptance of the Benjaminite's cursing and casting of stones hints at Jesus' acceptance of his scourging and other abuse at the hands of the Roman soldiers.

> " Inhumanity reaches new heights. Jesus is scourged and crowned with thorns. History is full of hatred and wars. Even today we witness acts of violence beyond belief: murder, violence to women and children, kidnapping, extortion, ethnic conflict, urban violence, physical and mental torture, violations of human rights.
>
> Jesus continues to suffer when believers are persecuted, when justice is distorted in court, corruption gets rooted, unjust structures grind the poor, minorities are suppressed, refugees and migrants are ill-treated. Jesus' garments are pulled away when the human person is put to shame on the screen, when women are compelled to humiliate themselves, when slum children go around in the streets picking up crumbs.
>
> Who are the guilty? Let us not point a finger at others, for we ourselves may have contributed a share to these forms of inhumanity.
>
> Lord Jesus, we know that it is you who suffer when we cause pain to each other and we remain indifferent. Your heart went out in compassion when you saw the crowds harassed and helpless.
>
> Most of all, may we share with the indigent your word of hope, your assurance of care. May zeal for your house burn in us like a fire. Help us to bring the sunshine of your joy into the lives of those who are trudging the path of despair. "
>
> —Pope Benedict XVI
> 6 April 2009

HERE IS THE MAN!

At the top of the window depicting Jesus being crowned with thorns is a pitcher and sponge, a foreshadowing of Jesus' thirsting on the cross.

Thirst is a common theme in both the Old and New Testaments, and the essential need for water would have been very much on the minds of people living in an arid climate.

The *Psalms* include such verses as these: "My soul thirsts for God, for the living God. When shall I come and behold the face of God?" (*Psalm* 42:2 [*Psalm* 42:3 NAB]) and "O God, you are my God, I seek you, my soul thirsts for you" (*Psalm* 63:1 [*Psalm* 63:2]). And the apostle John goes to some length to describe how during the last moments of his Passion Jesus says: "I thirst" (*John* 19:28). Jesus' thirst here is symbolic of the thirst of all humanity for God.

How do you think the experience of thirst functions as a suitable metaphor for spiritual longing? Describe a time in which you felt that God was satisfying your desire for union with him.

[handwritten notes, partially legible]

JOHN 19:2–11

²And the soldiers plaited a crown of thorns, and put it on his head, and clothed him in a purple robe; ³they came up to him, saying, "Hail, King of the Jews!" and struck him with their hands. ⁴Pilate went out again, and said to them, "Behold, I am bringing him out to you, that you may know that I find no crime in him." ⁵So Jesus came out, wearing the crown of thorns and the purple robe. Pilate said to them, "Here is the man!" ⁶When the chief priests and the officers saw him, they cried out, "Crucify him, crucify him!" Pilate said to them, "Take him yourselves and crucify him, for I find no crime in him." ⁷The Jews answered him, "We have a law, and by that law he ought to die, because he has made himself the Son of God!" ⁸When Pilate heard these words, he was even more afraid; ⁹he entered the praetorium again and said to Jesus, "Where are you from?" But Jesus gave no answer. ¹⁰Pilate therefore said to him, "You will not speak to me? Do you not know that I have power to release you, and power to crucify you?" ¹¹Jesus answered him, "You would have no power over me unless it had been given you from above; therefore he who delivered me to you has the greater sin."

1 After scourging Jesus, the Roman soldiers dress him in purple and place a crown of thorns on his head. This crown of thorns is included in nearly every artistic representation of Jesus' Crucifixion. Explain how the crown of thorns is related to the curse of Adam (*Genesis* 3:18) and to the sacrifice of Abraham (see *Genesis* 22:12–13).

thorns thistles shall eat by forth to you eat plants of field

2 In *John* 19:5, what is Pilate's response when he sees Jesus after the Roman soldiers have beaten and mocked Jesus and crowned him with thorns? In *John* 19:6, what statement does Pilate repeat concerning Jesus' crime (see *John* 18:38)?

Romans) Behold the man — Judge him yourselves." I find no guilt in him

3 Pilate clearly wants to release Jesus, but he also wants to do so without angering the Jews. In *John* 18:39, Pilate comes up with a plan to offer the crowd a Passover amnesty choice between Jesus and Barabbas. Why would Pilate have expected the crowd to choose to free Jesus? Why do you think that Pilate's plan failed?

Bitter brow

Custom to no guilt in him — release 1 prisoner to you @ Passover. Wanting to release

4 The Jews believe that Jesus is guilty of blasphemy. Paragraph 2148 of the *Catechism of the Catholic Church* teaches that blasphemy "consists in uttering against God—inwardly or outwardly—words of hatred, reproach, or defiance; in speaking ill of God; in failing in respect toward him in one's speech; in misusing God's name." Why do you think that Pilate becomes "even more afraid" when he is told that Jesus has made himself the Son of God?

Jew ought to die b/c made himself Son *Pilate loses either way*

5 In *John* 19:10, Pilate asks Jesus: "Do you not know that I have power to release you, and power to crucify you?" Who do you think has the real power in this situation (see *John* 10:17–18)? What is the extent of Pilate's power over Jesus? What power does Pilate have over the Jews seeking Jesus' crucifixion? *allowed*

I lay down my life in order to take it up again.

6 In the lower window that depicts an Old Testament parallel to Jesus being crowned with thorns, David has removed his crown to sing *Psalm* 51, which is known as the *Miserere*. How do you think that Jesus and David are similar in these window scenes? In what ways are they different? How are their two kingdoms related? What virtue or virtues do you think that both kings possess?

ec•ce ho•mo here is the man

When Pilate presents Jesus to the Jews, he announces: "Here is the man!" (*John* 19:5). In Latin, Pilate's words are **ecce homo**, and many artists have used them to label depictions of this scene. In *John's Gospel*, these words call to mind the curse of Adam, whose name means "the man." Although Pilate understands that Jesus is innocent, he fails to recognize that the suffering human standing before him is the Son of God, the new Adam, who through his Passion and death will cleanse all humanity of sin.

FRUITS OF PRAYER

REIGN OF CHRIST IN OUR HEARTS

The third Sorrowful Mystery is paired with the reign of Christ in the hearts of men and women, and also with the virtue of moral courage.

According to mystic Adrienne von Speyr (1902–1967), the mocking of Jesus is closely tied to the redemption of humanity: "He redeems sinners not by looking at some general, theoretical level of sin, but by looking at the concrete sins committed, in spirit and body. The servants who both mock and beat him thereby bind spirit and body so inseparably together that the two now can be redeemed together."

The King of all Creation allows himself to be crowned with sharp thorns and mocked. His unjust suffering moves Christians to ask forgiveness for the times that unloving thoughts, words, and actions have contributed to that pain and have mocked Christ's kingship.

As you meditate on this Mystery, offer each Hail Mary as a kiss on the thorn marks on Jesus' brow and ask him to reign in your heart as true King. Ask God to help you surrender your life to Jesus, and for the grace to follow his will in all areas of your life.

A sorrowful and repentant David sings the Miserere.

HAVE MERCY, O GOD

In the Old Testament parallel to the third Sorrowful Mystery, King David repents of some serious sins pointed out by the prophet Nathan. These include engaging in adultery with Bathsheba, a married woman, and then arranging for her husband to die in battle.

When David is called to answer for his actions, he responds with humility by removing his crown and royal robes, picking up his harp, and singing *Psalm* 51. *Sound healing*

This *Psalm* has become widely known as the *Miserere*, taking its Latin title from the opening words: "Have mercy on me, O God." The *Psalm* reflects David's deep sorrow at having offended God. His repentant attitude—"I know my transgressions, and my sin is ever before me"—illustrates the humility of his heart.

2 SAMUEL 12:7–10

⁷Nathan said to David, "You are the man. Thus says the Lᴏʀᴅ, the God of Israel, 'I anointed you king over Israel, and I delivered you out of the hand of Saul; ⁸and I gave you your master's house, and your master's wives into your bosom, and gave you the house of Israel and of Judah, and if this were too little, I would add to you as much more. ⁹Why have you despised the word of the Lᴏʀᴅ, to do what is evil in his sight? You have struck down Uriah the Hittite with the sword, and have taken his wife to be your wife, and have slain him with the sword of the Ammonites. ¹⁰Now therefore the sword shall never depart from your house....'"

PSALM 51:1–5

¹Have mercy on me, O God,
    according to your merciful love;
according to your abundant mercy
    blot out my transgressions.
²Wash me thoroughly from my iniquity,
    and cleanse me from my sin!
³For I know my transgressions,
    and my sin is ever before me.
⁴Against you, you only, have I sinned,
    and done that which is evil in your sight,
so that you are justified in your sentence
    and blameless in your judgment.
⁵Behold, I was brought forth in iniquity,
    and in sin did my mother conceive me.

7 Compare the prophet Nathan's words to David in *2 Samuel* 12:7 with Pilate's announcement to the Jews in *John* 19:5. Why do you think that Nathan is trying to get David to focus on his own human nature? What do you think Pilate's motivation is for emphasizing Jesus' humanity? Explain whether you think that pointing out Jesus' humanity makes the crowd sympathetic to Jesus. *More suffer*

Sympathy – Mercy – ✓

8 In *2 Samuel* 12:7–10, Nathan tells David that because of his adultery with Bathsheba and his murder of Uriah the Hittite, the sword shall never depart from David's house. How do you think that this Old Testament prophecy might have influenced the thinking of Jesus' followers who were looking for a messianic heir to the kingdom of David? In the New Testament, how does St. Paul's interpretation of the symbolism of a sword resemble the sword in Nathan's prophecy, and how is it different (see *Ephesians* 6:13–17)?

Sword Holy Spirit *of Spirit (word of God)*

9 What is David's response to Nathan's accusations (see *2 Samuel* 12:13)? What words would you use to describe the attitude David expresses toward God in *Psalm* 51, which is known as the *Miserere*? Explain whether you think that David is expressing an attitude common to a person who has just been accused of serious sin.

10 The punishment God inflicts on David as a result of David's sin is the death of the child born to him and the wife of Uriah. Read *2 Samuel* 12:15–18. What does David do to attempt to sway God's judgment? After the child has died, how does David's behavior change (see *2 Samuel* 12:19–23)? What is the name of the next child born to David and Bathsheba (see 2 *Samuel* 12:24–25)?

> **❝** Today we have been in spirit in the city of the "great King," who, as a sign of his kingship chose the crown of thorns rather than a royal crown....
>
> Was not Pilate right when—as he showed Christ to the people who were awaiting his condemnation in front of the praetorium "so that they might not be defiled, but might eat the Passover" (*John* 18:28)— he did not say "Here is the king" but "Here is the man" (*John* 19:5)?
>
> And in this way Pilate revealed the program of Christ's kingdom, which is to be free from the attributes of earthly power in order to reveal the thoughts of many hearts (*Luke* 2:35) and to bring near to them the Truth and Love that come from God. **❞**
>
> —Blessed John Paul II
> 13 April 1979

THE CROWN OF THORNS

Crowns developed to distinguish rulers of the people. Such rulers often are referred to as heads of state. As the human skull gradually came to be regarded as the location of the spirit, its dome shape suggested adornment with a circular crown.

The crown originally signified that God's power had been imparted to the person wearing it, and that person then was considered to be governing as God's representative. The points or floral shapes decorating a crown symbolize the light that accompanies power emanating from God.

Crowns usually are made of gold or other precious metal and are worn as a sign of honor. The Greeks crowned victors in athletic competitions with circlets made of laurel branches.

Jesus' crown of thorns is intended as an insult, however. The Roman soldiers are mocking Jesus' followers' hope that as Messiah Jesus also would be an imposing King of the Jews, like David, and therefore able to wield great political and military power. Instead, Jesus appears to be powerless before his enemies.

The truth of the matter remains hidden from the soldiers attempting to humiliate Jesus. Despite the soldiers' mocking, the crown of thorns has become one of the most recognized symbols in all of religious art. It is present on almost every depiction of Christ crucified, and it clearly identifies Jesus as a heavenly king—one who reigns through his shameful suffering on the cross.

HE WENT OUT, BEARING HIS OWN CROSS

In *John* 14:6, Jesus taught that he is "the way, the truth, and the life." While the third Sorrowful Mystery, the Crowning with Thorns, draws attention to the truth about Jesus' kingdom, the fourth Sorrowful Mystery draws attention to the spiritual life as a journey along the Way of the Cross.

Men and women who seek the truth will be able to pick up and embrace their own crosses in order to walk with Jesus on his path to Calvary. Jesus is the way (the method followed by Christians), the truth (our model of holiness), and the life (the ultimate goal of eternal salvation).

In the window showing Jesus carrying his cross, it fittingly is depicted as green (*Luke* 23:31), the color associated with springtime and spiritual growth. The green wood of the cross suggests regeneration and denotes the theological virtue of hope. The cross also frequently is referred to as the tree of life.

Review your own spiritual journey. Write down some of the most significant events, or stations, on your own Way of the Cross. What events have been particularly enlightening and led to a deeper relationship with Jesus? Were there any times that you especially felt Jesus' presence? Which spiritual landmarks in your life have nurtured the theological virtue of hope?

JOHN 19:12–17

[12]Upon this Pilate sought to release [Jesus], but the Jews cried out, "If you release this man, you are not Caesar's friend; every one who makes himself a king sets himself against Caesar." [13]When Pilate heard these words, he brought Jesus out and sat down on the judgment seat at a place called The Pavement, and in Hebrew, Gabbatha. [14]Now it was the day of Preparation of the Passover; it was about the sixth hour. He said to the Jews, "Here is your King!" [15]They cried out, "Away with him, away with him, crucify him!" Pilate said to them, "Shall I crucify your King?" The chief priests answered, "We have no king but Caesar." [16]Then he handed him over to them to be crucified.

[17]So they took Jesus, and he went out, bearing his own cross, to the place called the place of a skull, which is called in Hebrew Golgotha.

1 In *John* 19:12, Pilate once again tries to release Jesus. What do the Jewish religious leaders say that prevents Jesus' release, and why do you think that it is such an effective ploy?

2 The window depicting the fourth Sorrowful Mystery shows the Blessed Virgin Mary kneeling at Jesus' feet. Although the Gospels do not specifically state that Mary accompanied her Son along his route to Calvary, their meeting is one of the traditional Stations of the Cross. Read *John* 19:25. Explain whether you think this verse supports the view that Mary met Jesus on his Way of the Cross.

3 *Matthew* 27:32, *Mark* 15:21, and *Luke* 23:26 record that Simon of Cyrene was compelled by the Romans to help Jesus carry the cross. Why do you think the writers of these three Gospels felt it was important to include this detail? What possible reasons can you suggest for why this material is not included in *John's Gospel*?

4 In the Sermon on the Mount, Jesus advises his followers about how to respond if they are forced into temporary service. What is Jesus' advice to them (see *Matthew* 5:39–41)? What greater message do you think that Jesus might have been trying to get across?

VIA DOLOROSA

Via Dolorosa, or the Way of Sorrows, is the name given to the route taken by Jesus when he carried his cross from Jerusalem to Golgotha, the site of his Crucifixion.

On Fridays during Lent, and especially on Good Friday, Catholics around the world gather to pray the Stations of the Cross, meditating on key events in the final hours of Jesus' Passion. Through the prayers of the Stations of the Cross and other penitential prayers, Christians accompany Jesus on his road to Calvary.

The stained glass scene depicting the fourth Sorrowful Mystery of the Rosary shows Jesus meeting his Mother as he carries his cross along the Sorrowful Way. This is one of the Church's 14 traditionally recognized Stations of the Cross, but along with the number of times that Jesus fell, and with Veronica wiping his face with her veil, this meeting between Jesus and his Mother is not recorded in Scripture. These events have been a topic of meditation for Christians since the earliest days of the Church, however, and numerous pilgrims to Jerusalem have stopped to pray at the traditional site of the fourth Station of the Cross.

In *Rosarium Virginis Mariae*, Blessed John Paul II taught that by meditating in prayer on such individual moments of Jesus' Passion, Christians can find "the culmination of the revelation of God's love and the source of our salvation."

PATIENCE IN TRIALS

The fruit or virtue paired with the fourth Sorrowful Mystery is patience in trials. Focusing on the need for patience during difficult situations is fitting when contemplating Jesus' Way of Sorrows.

Before Jesus is forced to carry his cross, he already has been subjected to a disappointing turn of events and has suffered a number of indignities and degradations. He experiences agony in the garden knowing what is to befall him. He is betrayed by Judas and abandoned by his friends. He is tried unjustly, scourged, and mocked.

Yet despite all of these sufferings, and in a debilitated physical condition, Jesus courageously carries on and embraces the cross. He perseveres in love as he carries his heavy cross up Calvary.

How often do you give up and lose patience when times are tough or when you are tired or busy with the details of life?

As you meditate on this Mystery, ask for the grace to courageously face your own trials and for the strength to persevere in joining your faith journey to Jesus' Way of the Cross as he trod to his Crucifixion.

David weeps as he climbs the Mount of Olives.

DAVID ASCENDS THE MOUNT OF OLIVES

The Old Testament parallel to Jesus carrying his cross is David, weeping and barefoot, climbing the Mount of Olives.

The scene takes place as David is fleeing Jerusalem to escape from his son Absalom, who has turned against his father. David's supporters include priests bearing the ark of the covenant. They are attempting to follow their king into the wilderness.

David sends the priests back to Jerusalem, however, saying: "Carry the ark of God back into the city. If I find favor in the eyes of the LORD, he will bring me back and let me see both it and his habitation; but if he says, 'I have no pleasure in you,' behold, here I am, let him do to me what seems good to him."

Although David is tearful to be leaving Jerusalem, he maintains an attitude of total reliance on the will of God.

2 SAMUEL 15:24–30

24And Abiathar came up, and behold, Zadok came also, with all the Levites, bearing the ark of the covenant of God; and they set down the ark of God, until the people had all passed out of the city. 25Then the king said to Zadok, "Carry the ark of God back into the city. If I find favor in the eyes of the LORD, he will bring me back and let me see both it and his habitation; 26but if he says, 'I have no pleasure in you,' behold, here I am, let him do to me what seems good to him." 27The king also said to Zadok the priest, "Look, go back to the city in peace, you and Abiathar, with your two sons, Ahimaaz your son, and Jonathan the son of Abiathar. 28See, I will wait at the fords of the wilderness until word comes from you to inform me." 29So Zadok and Abiathar carried the ark of God back to Jerusalem, and they remained there.

30But David went up the ascent of the Mount of Olives, weeping as he went, barefoot and with his head covered; and all the people who were with him covered their heads, and they went up, weeping as they went.

5 Paragraph 2708 of the *Catechism of the Catholic Church* teaches that Christian meditation can help "deepen our convictions of faith, prompt the conversion of our heart, and strengthen our will to follow Christ." What do you think there is about reliving Jesus' suffering that increases faith and leads men and women to become more active in their spiritual lives? Describe a situation in which you or someone close to you experienced spiritual renewal as a direct result of suffering. Think of someone you know who is suffering right now. What can you do to ease that person's pain?

6 In *2 Samuel* 15:24, Zadok the priest and the Levites carry the ark of the covenant of God outside Jerusalem and set it down until all the people following King David have passed out of the city. Explain what might have been the purpose of this action, which echoes the Israelites passing over the Jordan River to enter the Promised Land (see *Joshua* 3:1—4:18).

7 In *2 Samuel* 15:25–27, what does King David instruct Zadok to do with the ark? What accomplishment in David's past might have contributed to his decision, and why (see *2 Samuel* 6:12–19)?

8 Compare David's emotional state in *2 Samuel* 6:12–19, when he brought the ark of the covenant into Jerusalem, with his emotional state in *2 Samuel* 15:30, when he orders it returned to the Holy City. What is the mood of the people in each instance? Explain whether you think that the people are supportive of King David or whether they would prefer to see Absalom come into power.

9 Why do you think that David removes his shoes and covers his head to climb the Mount of Olives? List some of the ways that David's ascent resembles Jesus' carrying his cross up Calvary.

10 Under what condition does David expect to be able to return to Jerusalem (see *2 Samuel* 15:25)? In whose hands does David's fate rest? What do David's words to Zadok indicate about David's relationship with God? What do they suggest about David's feelings concerning Jerusalem? Explain whether you think that David trusts Zadok and the priests.

---

as•ce•sis self-discipline

Ascesis is the practice of penance, mortification, and self-denial to promote greater self-mastery and to foster the way of perfection by embracing the way of the cross. Although **ascesis** is difficult, the Church teaches that it has its rewards. Paragraph 2015 of the *Catechism of the Catholic Church* explains: "Spiritual progress entails the **ascesis** and mortification that gradually lead to living in the peace and joy of the Beatitudes."

> **"**Lent is a journey, it means accompanying Jesus who goes up to Jerusalem, the place of the fulfilment of his mystery of Passion, death, and Resurrection. It reminds us that Christian life is a "way" to take, not so much consistent with a law to observe as with the very person of Christ....
>
> In the Church's tradition, this journey we are asked to take in Lent is marked by certain practices: fasting, almsgiving, and prayer. Fasting means abstinence from food but includes other forms of privation for a more modest life. However, all this is not yet the full reality of fasting. It is an outer sign of an inner reality, of our commitment, with God's help, to abstain from evil and to live by the Gospel. Those who are unable to nourish themselves with the word of God do not fast properly.
>
> In the Christian tradition fasting is closely linked to almsgiving. St. Leo the Great taught: "All that each Christian is bound to do in every season he must now do with greater solicitude and devotion in order to fulfill the apostolic prescription of Lenten fasting consistently, not only in abstinence from food but also and above all from sin. Furthermore, with this holy fasting that is only right, no work may be more fruitfully associated than almsgiving, which under the one name of 'mercy,' embraces many good works.**"**
>
> —Pope Benedict XVI
> 9 March 2011

JOHN 19:18–35

[18]There they crucified him, and with him two others, one on either side, and Jesus between them. [19]Pilate also wrote a title and put it on the cross; it read, "Jesus of Nazareth, the King of the Jews." [20]Many of the Jews read this title, for the place where Jesus was crucified was near the city; and it was written in Hebrew, in Latin, and in Greek. [21]The chief priests of the Jews then said to Pilate, "Do not write, 'The King of the Jews,' but, 'This man said, I am King of the Jews.'" [22]Pilate answered, "What I have written I have written."

[23]When the soldiers had crucified Jesus they took his garments and made four parts, one for each soldier; also his tunic. But the tunic was without seam, woven from top to bottom; [24]so they said to one another, "Let us not tear it, but cast lots for it to see whose it shall be." This was to fulfil the Scripture,

"They parted my garments among them,
and for my clothing they cast lots."

[25]So the soldiers did this. But standing by the cross of Jesus were his mother, and his mother's sister, Mary the wife of Clopas, and Mary Magdalene. [26]When Jesus saw his mother, and the disciple whom he loved standing near, he said to his mother, "Woman, behold, your son!" [27]Then he said to the disciple, "Behold, your mother!" And from that hour the disciples took her to his own home.

[28]After this Jesus, knowing that all was now finished, said (to fulfil the Scripture), "I thirst." [29]A bowl full of vinegar stood there; so they put a sponge full of the vinegar on hyssop and held it to his mouth. [30]When Jesus had received the vinegar, he said, "It is finished"; and he bowed his head and gave up his spirit.

[31]Since it was the day of Preparation, in order to prevent the bodies from remaining on the cross on the sabbath (for that sabbath was a high day), the Jews asked Pilate that their legs might be broken, and that they might be taken away. [32]So the soldiers came and broke the legs of the first, and of the other who had been crucified with him; [33]but when they came to Jesus and saw that he was already dead, they did not break his legs. [34]But one of the soldiers pierced his side with a spear, and at once there came out blood and water. [35]He who saw it has borne witness—his testimony is true, and he knows that he tells the truth—that you also may believe.

THERE THEY CRUCIFIED HIM

At the top of the Crucifixion Window is a nest with a pelican and several newly hatched baby birds. Because the pelican was believed to feed its young by piercing its own side, this bird has become an image of Jesus, who gives himself as food in the sacrament of the Eucharist.

St. Thomas Aquinas, speaking for the Church, taught that the understanding that in this sacrament are the true Body of Christ and his true Blood is possible only by faith. List ways in which you feel nourished when you receive the Eucharist.

1 The INRI seen on many crucifixes comes from the first letters of the Latin words of the sign Pilate had placed on the cross: "Jesus of Nazareth, the King of the Jews" (*John* 19:19). What do you think Pilate's motivation was for having the sign written in the first place, and why do you think that he had it written in those three languages?

2 In *John* 19:21–22, what change do the Jews want Pilate to make in the sign's wording, and why do you think that Pilate refuses?

THE PLACE OF THE SKULL

The site of Jesus' Crucifixion was Golgatha, a word that in Hebrew means "place of the skull" (*John* 19:17). Apocryphal tradition holds that Golgatha marked the exact center of the Earth. In addition, this site was believed to be the final resting place for Adam's remains, which were said to have been taken there by Noah and Melchizedek after they were shown the way by an angel.

The skull and crossbones that appear at the foot of the cross in the Crucifixion Window represent these physical remains of Adam, which in turn represent the mortality of all humanity. The bones' position relative to the cross is intended to signify that Jesus' blood flowing over them opens the door to salvation for all men and women.

The skull and crossbones at the foot of the cross also symbolize the bodily resurrection foretold by Ezekiel in his prophecy of dried bones coming to life: "Therefore prophesy, and say to them, 'Thus says the Lord GOD: Behold I will open your graves, and raise you up from your graves, O my people; and I will bring you home into the land of Israel'" (*Ezekiel* 37:12).

FRUITS OF PRAYER

SELF-SACRIFICE

Meditating on Jesus' Crucifixion, the fifth Sorrowful Mystery, is tied to the fruit of self-sacrifice. It also is related to the virtues of forgiving others and of self-denial.

St. Ephrem the Syrian (306–373) explained how Jesus' self-sacrifice is able to bring about the possibility of salvation for humanity: "He who was the carpenter's glorious Son set up his cross above death's all-consuming jaws, and led the human race into the dwelling place of life. Since a tree had brought about the downfall of mankind, it was upon a tree that mankind crossed over to the realm of life.... We give glory to you, Lord, who raised up your cross to span the jaws of death like a bridge by which souls might pass from the region of the dead to the land of the living."

While not every Christian will be called to the imitate Jesus in the martyrdom of physical death, all Christian men and women are called to imitate his self-sacrifice. Pray for the grace to die to your own desires and to fill the emptiness of your life with love for others. Ask Jesus to show you acts of kindness you can perform that involve self-denial and forgiveness.

Psalm 22 is inspired by David's vision of Christ crucified.

DAVID'S VISION

The lower Crucifixion Window shows David's vision of the crucified Christ, which is recorded in the words of *Psalm 22*. It is a prayerful plea for deliverance from suffering.

David kneels with his breast bared before his vision of a radiant cross on which Jesus is being crucified. David's crown and scepter rest at his feet. These symbols provide a reminder that Jesus is a descendant of the royal house of David and the promised Messiah destined to rule over Israel for all eternity.

crux cross

The Latin word for cross, **crux**, has come to mean the decisive or most important point of an issue, or a point of difficulty.

PSALM 22:1–8, 16–18

¹My God, my God, why have you forsaken me?
Why are you so far from helping me,
from the words of my groaning?
²O my God, I cry by day,
but you do not answer;
and by night, but find no rest.
³Yet you are holy, enthroned on the praises
of Israel.
⁴In you our fathers trusted;
they trusted, and you delivered them.
⁵To you they cried, and were saved;
in you they trusted, and were
not disappointed.
⁶But I am a worm, and no man;

scorned by men, and despised by the people.
⁷All who see me mock at me,
they make mouths at me, they
wag their heads;
⁸He committed his cause to the
Lord; let him deliver him,
let him rescue him, for he delights in him! ...
¹⁶Yes, dogs are round about me;
a company of evildoers encircle me;
they have pierced my hands and feet—
¹⁷I can count all my bones—
they stare and gloat over me;
¹⁸they divide my garments among them,
and for my clothing they cast lots.

3 Read *Psalm* 22, a plea for deliverance from suffering. Which verse foreshadows the actions of the Roman soldiers in *John* 19:23–24? (Verse in *Psalm* 22 will vary in the NAB.) List examples of other events connected with Jesus' Passion that are foreshadowed in *Psalm* 22.

4 According to *John* 19:25, who is at the foot of Jesus' cross? *John* 19:26 includes the additional information that the disciple "whom [Jesus] loved" also was present. What does this suggest about the authenticity of the Crucifixion account in *John's Gospel*?

5 The Church understands that *John* 19:26–27 describes Jesus' gift of his Mother to be Mother of the Church (see *CCC* 963—*CCC* 970). List as many titles as you know for the Blessed Virgin Mary—Immaculate Conception, Our Lady of Sorrows, etc.—and explain how these titles reflect Mary's maternal role in the Church.

6 *John* 19:34 records that blood and water flow when Jesus' side is pierced. Why does one of the soldiers pierce Jesus?

7 In *John* 19:35, John goes way out of his way to point out that he is an eyewitness to Jesus' piercing. What does John write that he hopes to achieve by repeating this detail? How does the Church interpret the blood and water in *John* 19:34 (see *CCC* 1225)?

8 Christian tradition looks at all of the *Psalms* in the light of Christ, and *Psalm* 22 is understood to be a vision of Jesus crucified. Why do you think that David is chosen to receive this vision?

9 *Matthew* 27:46 and *Mark* 15:34 record Jesus on the cross quoting *Psalm* 22:1 (*Psalm* 22:2 NAB). Compare *Psalm* 22:1–2 (*Psalm* 22:2–3 NAB) with *Psalm* 22:23–31 (*Psalm* 22:24–32 NAB). How can you reconcile the difference in tone between the opening and the conclusion? Do you think that Jesus feels abandoned by God?

10 *Luke* 23:46 records that Jesus' last words from the cross are: "Father, into your hands I commit my spirit!" from *Psalm* 31:5 (*Psalm* 31:6 NAB). It was Jewish practice to teach this *Psalm* to children as a bedtime prayer, much like children today learn "Now I lay me down to sleep." Many monks repeat *Psalm* 31:5 (*Psalm* 31:6 NAB) as part of their final prayers of the day. Read all of *Psalm* 31. In quoting from this *Psalm*, what point do you think that Jesus was trying to make for the benefit of those witnessing his Crucifixion?

> " Jesus and, in his footsteps, his Sorrowful Mother and the saints, are witnesses who show us how to experience the tragedy of suffering for our own good and for the salvation of the world.
>
> There is more. Because the Son of God wanted freely to embrace suffering and death, we are also capable of seeing God's image in the face of those who suffer. This preferential love of the Lord for those who are suffering helps us to see others more clearly and to give them, above and beyond their material demands, the look of love that they need. This can only happen as the fruit of a personal encounter with Christ.
>
> Every human being is called to the greatness of showing compassion and loving concern to the suffering, just as God himself did.
>
> In a mysterious yet real way, the presence of the suffering awakens in our often hardened hearts a tenderness that opens us to salvation. In a decisive way Christians offer the Lord their lives, cooperating with him and somehow becoming part of the treasury of compassion so greatly needed by the human race. "
> —Pope Benedict XVI
> 20 August 2011

A PSALM OF HOPE

Psalm 22 contains many parallels to Jesus' Passion, and Jesus quotes the first verse from the cross: "My God, my God, why have you forsaken me?" (*Matthew* 27:46). Although Jesus expresses a feeling of being abandoned, *Psalm* 22 ends on a note of hope: "All the ends of the earth shall remember and turn to the LORD; and all the families of nations shall worship before him" (*Psalm* 22:27 [*Psalm* 22:28 NAB]).

THEY WENT TO THE TOMB WHEN THE SUN HAD RISEN

At the top of the Resurrection Window a phoenix rises triumphantly from its nest of flames. Ancient cultures associated the firebird with eternal rebirth. It became a symbol of Christ's Resurrection because the phoenix was said to set its nest on fire and then return to life after three days.

Both the phoenix and Christianity speak to humanity's desire to escape death. While the phoenix is a mythical creature, Christianity is founded on belief in Jesus Christ as the Son of God, and on the truth that Jesus did in fact conquer death in order to open the way to eternal life for all men and women.

In what ways has the Christian belief that it is possible to live forever affected the way you think about your life on earth?

MARK 16:1–11

[1]And when the sabbath was past, Mary Magdalene, and Mary the mother of James, and Salome, bought spices, so that they might go and anoint him. [2]And very early on the first day of the week they went to the tomb when the sun had risen. [3]And they were saying to one another, "Who will roll away the stone for us from the door of the tomb?" [4]And looking up, they saw that the stone was rolled back; for it was very large. [5]And entering the tomb, they saw a young man sitting on the right side, dressed in a white robe, and they were amazed. [6]And he said to them, "Do not be amazed; you seek Jesus of Nazareth, who was crucified. He has risen, he is not here; see the place where they laid him. [7]But go, tell his disciples and Peter that he is going before you to Galilee; there you will see him, as he told you." [8]And they went out and fled from the tomb; for trembling and astonishment had come upon them; and they said nothing to any one, for they were afraid.

[9]Now when he rose early on the first day of the week, he appeared first to Mary Magdalene, from whom he had cast out seven demons. [10]She went and told those who had been with him, as they mourned and wept. [11]But when they heard that he was alive and had been seen by her, they would not believe it.

1 In *Mark* 16:1–4, what day of the week is it when Mary Magdalene, Mary the mother of James, and Salome go to Jesus' tomb? What time of day is it? For what purpose are the women going there? Why do you think that none of the disciples are accompanying them?

[handwritten: monday]
[handwritten: ☀ womans work ☀]
[handwritten: spice Embalm]

2 One of the main concerns of the women is that they will be unable to roll the large, heavy stone away from the entrance to the tomb. When the women arrive, however, they find the stone already rolled back. Who do you think moved the stone? *[handwritten: God that]*

3 In *Mark* 16:5, when the women enter the tomb, they see a young man sitting on the right side of the tomb. What does the man's attire suggest about who he is and what his purpose there might be? Why do you think that Mark includes the detail that this young man was sitting on the "right side" of the tomb?

4 In *Mark* 16:6, the young man tells the women that Jesus is not in the tomb, something they probably could see for themselves. According to the young man, what has happened to Jesus? Explain whether you think that the women believe the young man or understand what they are being told about Jesus.

HE IS RISEN!

The Resurrection Window depicts what paragraph 638 of the *Catechism of the Catholic Church* describes as "the crowning truth" of the Christian faith: that Jesus Christ has conquered death.

The risen Jesus appears standing above his tomb, and soldiers posted to guard it sleep nearby. The sleeping soldiers call attention to Peter's understanding that Jesus is the "Son of the living God" (*Matthew* 16:16).

It is common for people to refer to the dead as "being asleep." In *John* 11:11 Jesus says: "Our friend Lazarus has fallen asleep, but I go to awake him out of sleep." Jesus is misunderstood by his disciples, who think that Lazarus is merely dozing until Jesus spells it out more clearly for them: "Larazus is dead" (*John* 11:14).

When Lazarus is raised from the dead after being in the tomb four days, Scripture records that "the dead man came out, his hands and feet bound with bandages, and his face wrapped with a cloth. Jesus said to them, 'unbind him, and let him go'" (*John* 11:44). The risen Jesus, however, is depicted coming forth from the grave completely unbound and carrying a victory banner.

In *Revelation* 1:18, the risen Jesus takes an almost-laid back attitude towards death, telling John: "I died, and behold I am alive for evermore." It is easy to miss Jesus' point and the ramifications it has for all Christians. For Jesus, death no longer is a big deal.

FAITH

The fruit associated with the first Glorious Mystery, the Resurrection, is faith. In *Porta Fidei,* the apostolic letter announcing the Year of Faith, Pope Benedict XVI refers to the "door of faith" mentioned in *Acts* 14:27, writing that this door always is open for humanity. The door of faith ushers men and women into the life of communion with God through entry into his Church.

On Easter morning the women are concerned about who will roll away the heavy stone from the tomb, but when they arrive they find it already rolled back. Looking inside, they see that the tomb is empty. As news of his Resurrection spreads, Jesus' followers find the faith that their hearts have been seeking. The night of loss and sadness is brightened by the light of new life and joy.

In *Porta Fidei,* Pope Benedict XVI defines faith as an intimate relationship with Christ, who enables Christians to open their hearts to this mystery of divine love and to live as men and women conscious of being loved by God.

As you meditate on the Glorious Mystery of Jesus' Resurrection, ask God to open wide the door of your heart and to increase your faith.

Three figures walk unharmed in the fiery furnace.

OUR GOD IS ABLE TO DELIVER US

Fire figures prominently in the lower Resurrection Window, which depicts Shadrach, Meshach, and Abednego in the blazing furnace. Only two of those Old Testament characters appear in the stained glass scene, however.

The glowing third figure shown is that of the mysterious fourth person who was seen walking unhurt in the midst of the fire with the other three men.

King Nebuchadnezzar, describing this fourth figure, said he appeared to be "like a son of the gods."

Shadrach, Meshach, and Abednego were thrown into the furnace for refusing to worship Babylonian gods or an image made of gold. Instead, they expressed supreme confidence in the God of Israel, saying, "Our God whom we serve is able to deliver us from the burning fiery furnace."

DANIEL 3:16–20, 24–25

[16]Shadrach, Meshach, and Abednego answered the king, "O Nebuchadnezzar, we have no need to answer you in this matter. [17]If it be so, our God whom we serve is able to deliver us from the burning fiery furnace; and he will deliver us out of your hand, O king. [18]But if not, be it known to you, O king, that we will not serve your gods or worship the golden image which you have set up."

[19]Then Nebuchadnezzar was full of fury, and the expression of his face was changed against Shadrach, Meshach, and Abednego. He ordered the furnace heated seven times more than it was accustomed to be heated. [20]And he ordered certain mighty men of his army to bind Shadrach, Meshach, and Abednego, and to cast them into the burning fiery furnace....

[24]Then King Nebuchadnezzar was astonished and rose up in haste. He said to his counselors, "Did we not cast three men bound into the fire?" They answered the king, "True, O king." [25]He answered, "But I see four men loose, walking in the midst of the fire, and they are not hurt; and the appearance of the fourth is like a son of the gods."

5 In *Mark* 16:7, what instructions does the young man give the women? How do the women respond? What in Mark's account suggests that all of the women present may not immediately have followed the young man's instructions? *fear*

Does believe her

6 What does Mark write about Mary Magdalene in *Mark* 16:9–11 that sets her apart from the other women who went to the tomb? Compare Mark's account of Mary Magdalene's encounter at the tomb with her experience described in *John* 20:11–18. What do you think might explain the difference between the two accounts? *angels' "peace be with you"*

7 In *Mark* 16:10, what are the disciples doing when Mary Magdalene tells them that she has seen Jesus alive? Why do you think that the disciples do not believe her? Why do you think that John fails to include that information in his account of Mary Magdalene's report to the disciples?

8 Read *Matthew* 28:11–15, which tells how the chief priests and elders in Jerusalem decide to deal with the news of Jesus' Resurrection. What is the plan that these Jewish religious leaders come up with? Explain whether you think that it was a good idea.

9 Read *Daniel* 3:1–25 (*Daniel* 3:1–23, 91–92 NAB). Why are Shadrach, Meshach, and Abednego thrown into the furnace? Do you think that reason constitutes a valid principle for which to die? *angel of flames safe*

10 What is the outcome for Shadrach, Meshach, and Abednego? How do they avoid perishing? In *Daniel* 3:28 (*Daniel* 3:95 NAB), who does King Nebuchadnezzar credit with saving them? In *Daniel* 3:29 (*Daniel* 3:96 NAB), what punishment is ordered by the king for anyone speaking against the three men or their God?

> " Faith in the risen Christ transforms life, bringing about within us a continuous resurrection, as St. Paul wrote to the first believers: "For once you were darkness, but now you are light in the Lord; walk as children of light (for the fruit of light is found in all that is good and right and true)" (*Ephesians* 5:8–9).
>
> In the Resurrection of Jesus a new condition of being human begins, which illumines and transforms our daily routine and opens a qualitatively different and new future to humanity as a whole.... And this is not only the way to transform ourselves, but also to transform the world, to give the earthly city a new face that will encourage the development of humanity and of society, in accordance with the logic of solidarity and of goodness, in profound respect for the dignity proper to each. "
> —Pope Benedict XVI
> 27 April 2011

Sep•tu•a•gint
Greek Old Testament

This Greek version of the Hebrew Scriptures incorporates many of the oldest of several ancient translations of the Old Testament. The deuterocanonical works in Catholic Bibles, often called the apocrypha by Protestants, come from the **Septuagint.** This includes the additional 68 verses that are inserted between *Daniel* 3:23 and 3:24 in the RSV (*Daniel* 3.23 and 3:91 in the NAB).

THE FIERY FURNACE

In Daniel's account of Shadrach, Meshach, and Abednego's experience, the fiery furnace is intended to be a cause of death for those who have antagonized King Nebuchadnezzar.

The fiery furnace serves as an obvious Old Testament type of the punishment Jesus speaks of in the New Testament when describing the final Judgment: "Then [the King] will say to those at his left hand,' Depart from me, you cursed, into the eternal fire prepared for the devil and his angels'" (*Matthew* 25:41).

The mysterious fourth figure walking amid the flames is described by Nebuchadnezzar as having an appearance "like a son of the gods," and this figure clearly is responsible for protecting Shadrach, Meshach, and Abednego. He is an obvious type of Jesus, the Son of God, who in the New Testament brings salvation and is able to deliver his followers from eternal destruction symbolized by fire (*Revelation* 20:14–15).

WHY DO YOU STAND LOOKING INTO HEAVEN?

As the disciples stand watching, the risen Jesus is lifted up and taken away on a cloud. In the Ascension Window, Jesus is shown being taken up into heaven with his right hand raised in blessing.

During his time living among men and women, Jesus had insisted on the importance of his return to the Father: "Truly, truly, I say to you, he who believes in me will also do the works that I do; and greater works than these will he do, because I go to the Father. Whatever you ask in my name, I will do it, that the Father may be glorified in the Son; if you ask anything in my name, I will do it" (*John* 14:12–14).

On Holy Thursday of 2012, Pope Benedict XVI preached that Jesus' "exodus" to heaven was entirely for the benefit of sinful humanity: "It was for us that he came down from heaven and for us that he ascended into heaven … after having touched the abyss of the maximal distance from God."

Through the words of the two men in white robes, Jesus invites his followers not to stand around looking into the sky but to be joined together in prayer to invoke the Holy Spirit.

Who serves as the most credible witness of faith for you? This week as you meditate on the Mystery of the Ascension, invoke the Holy Spirit for the power to be an effective witness.

ACTS 1:6–11

[6]So when they had come together, they asked him, "Lord, will you at this time restore the kingdom to Israel?" [7]He said to them, "It is not for you to know times or seasons which the Father has fixed by his own authority. [8]But you shall receive power when the Holy Spirit has come upon you; and you shall be my witnesses in Jerusalem and in all Judea and Samaria and to the end of the earth." [9]And when he had said this, as they were looking on, he was lifted up, and a cloud took him out of their sight. [10]And while they were gazing into heaven as he went, behold, two men stood by them in white robes, [11]and said, "Men of Galilee, why do you stand looking into heaven? This Jesus, who was taken up from you into heaven, will come in the same way as you saw him go into heaven."

1 In *Acts* 1:6, the question on the minds of Jesus' disciples has to do with restoration of the kingdom of Israel. Why do you think that the disciples are asking Jesus about a kingdom now? How did Jesus react to pressure to make him king prior to his Passion (see *John* 6:15)? Explain whether you think that the events surrounding Jesus' Passion, death, and Resurrection have changed the disciples' understanding of the nature of Jesus' kingship.

2 In *Acts* 1:7–8, Jesus' response to his disciples' concern about the restoration of the kingdom of Israel is a rather diplomatic form of "It's none of your business." Who does Jesus say has authority over when such a restoration might occur? What does Jesus' promise that the disciples will receive power from the Holy Spirit indicate about his understanding of what it is that interests them?

3 What does Jesus say that he wants the disciples to do after the Holy Spirit has come upon them? How far does he expect them to travel in order to accomplish their task? What do these instructions imply about what Jesus considers to be the geographical boundaries of the kingdom of Israel?

4 Compare Jesus' last words to the disciples before his Ascension in *Acts* 1:7–8 with his last post-Resurrection words recorded in *Matthew* 28:16–20. How are the two accounts similar? How are they different? What evidence can you find to indicate that both events took place in Galilee? Why do you think that none of the Gospels include an account of the Ascension?

5 In *Acts* 1:9, how is Jesus taken into heaven? Explain whether you think that the disciples were expecting to see this happen.

6 Who do you think the two men are who suddenly appear in *Acts* 1:10? What does their attire indicate about where they might have come from? What question do they ask the disciples, and what reassuring words do they have for Jesus' followers who have just seen him lifted up out of their sight?

Chi•Rho monogram for Christ

At the top of the Ascension Window is the **Chi-Rho**, a monogram for Christ that is created by superimposing the first two letters of the Greek spelling of the word Christ. The use of the **Chi-Rho** additionally can denote triumph over an enemy through divine assistance. The Roman emperor Constantine, having dreamed of conquering under the Christian symbol of a cross, won an important battle after having the **Chi-Rho** placed on all of his military banners. This led to acceptance of Christianity as an official religion of the Roman empire.

HOPE

The second Glorious Mystery of the Rosary is the Ascension. Pope Benedict XVI, in his Ascension 2012 homily, called it "the last act of our liberation from sin," which "not only proclaims the immortality of the soul, but also that of the flesh."

The fruit associated with the Mystery of Jesus' Ascension is the theological virtue of hope. This Mystery also is associated with the desire for heaven, a closely related concept.

After the disciples return home following Jesus' Ascension, they have to hope that he will indeed be with them "always, to the close of the age" (*Matthew* 28:20). Even though they do not yet understand exactly how that will happen, they maintain hope that they will be able to be Jesus' witnesses and will be able to carry out the mission that he has given them. They cling to the hope that they will one day see Jesus face to face in heaven.

How do you think that hope is able to help you through such tough times as illness or the death of a loved one? As you meditate on the Mystery of the Ascension, ask God to grant you an increase in the virtue of hope.

A chariot of fire takes the prophet Elijah up into heaven.

ELIJAH WENT UP BY A WHIRLWIND

The lower Ascension Window depicts the prophet Elijah's ascent into heaven by means of a chariot of fire.

Considered to be Israel's greatest prophet, Elijah frequently appears in art and literature as a representation of all the prophets. He is credited with performing many mighty deeds, including raising a widow's son to life.

He also slew 400 prophets of the false god Baal, which incurred the wrath of Queen Jezebel, who sought to have him killed. Elijah fled from her, and his self-imposed exile in the wilderness (*1 Kings* 19:1–4) can be seen as a foreshadowing of Jesus' agony in the Garden of Gethsemane.

2 KINGS 2:6–14

⁶Then Elijah said to him, "Tarry here, I beg you, for the LORD has sent me to the Jordan." But he said, "As the LORD lives, and as you yourself live, I will not leave you." So the two of them went on. ⁷Fifty men of the sons of the prophets also went, and stood at some distance from them, as they both were standing by the Jordan. ⁸Then Elijah took his coat, and rolled it up, and struck the water, and the water was parted to the one side and to the other, till the two of them could go over on dry ground.

⁹When they had crossed, Elijah said to Elisha, "Ask what I shall do for you, before I am taken from you." And Elisha said, "I beg you, let me inherit a double share of your spirit." ¹⁰And he said, "You have asked a hard thing; yet, if you see me as I am being taken from you, it shall be so for you; but if you do not see me, it shall not be so." ¹¹And as they still went on and talked, behold, a chariot of fire and horses of fire separated the two of them. And Elijah went up by a whirlwind into heaven. ¹²And Elisha saw it and he cried, "My father, my father! the chariots of Israel and its horsemen!" And he saw him no more.

Then he took hold of his own clothes and tore them in two pieces. ¹³And he took up the coat of Elijah that had fallen from him, and went back and stood on the bank of the Jordan. ¹⁴Then he took the coat of Elijah that had fallen from him, and struck the water, saying, "Where is the LORD, the God of Elijah?" And when he had struck the water, the water was parted to the one side and to the other; and Elisha went over.

7 The primary job of a prophet is to speak for God. *Sirach* 48:1 characterizes Elijah as arising "like a fire, and his word burned like a torch." Against whom does God send Elijah to speak and for what purpose (see *1 Kings* 18:17–19)? Why do you think that the author of Sirach compares Elijah's words to fire?

8 In *Luke* 12:49, Jesus says: "I came to cast fire upon the earth; and would that it were already kindled!" Explain why Jesus might want to cast fire on the earth (see *Luke* 3:16). According to Church teaching, how is fire connected with the Holy Spirit (see *CCC* 696)?

9 Compare the account of Elijah being taken into heaven (*2 Kings* 2:6–14) with the account of the Israelites crossing the Red Sea (*Exodus* 14:1–29) and then entering the Promised Land (*Joshua* 3:1–17). How are these events similar? How are they different? In what ways does Elijah resemble Moses? In what ways does Elisha resemble Joshua? Why do you think it might be fitting that Elijah crosses the Jordan River before he is taken to heaven?

10 Read *1 Kings* 18:20–40, which recounts Elijah's triumph over the prophets of Baal through use of fire and water. According to Church teaching, how does water symbolize the Holy Spirit (see *CCC* 694)? Why do you think it might be fitting that Elijah be taken to heaven in a chariot of fire? Explain which symbol of the Holy Spirit—fire or water—you think is more important in drawing a parallel between Elijah being taken to heaven and Jesus' Ascension.

ELISHA'S INHERITANCE

After Elijah's ascent, his servant Elisha inherits a double portion of the prophet's spirit, in an act that the Church fathers see as a foreshadowing of Jesus sending the Holy Spirit to his disciples after his Ascension. The Church recognizes in this Old Testament event a reflection of the many varied spiritualities that have developed throughout history to bear witness to the vast number of saints who serve as models of holiness for the faithful.

Paragraph 2684 of the *Catechism of the Catholic Church* teaches that when Elijah's spirit is passed to Elisha this constitutes a share in the living tradition of prayer that falls under the guidance of the Holy Spirit: "The personal charism of some witnesses to God's love for men has been handed on, like 'the spirit' of Elijah to Elisha and John the Baptist, so that their followers may have a share in this spirit....The different schools of Christian spirituality share in the living tradition of prayer and are essential guides for the faithful. In their rich diversity they are refractions of the one pure light of the Holy Spirit."

❝ He was lifted up" (*Acts* 1:9): This expression corresponds to the sensible and spiritual experience of the apostles. It refers to an upward movement, to a passage from earth to heaven, especially as a sign of another "passage"—Christ passes to the glorified state in God. The first meaning of the Ascension is precisely this: a revelation that the risen one has entered the heavenly intimacy of God. That is proved by "the cloud," a biblical sign of the divine presence. Christ disappears from the eyes of his disciples by entering the transcendent sphere of the invisible God.

This last consideration is a further confirmation of the meaning of the mystery that is Jesus Christ's Ascension into heaven. The Son who "came forth from the Father and came into the world, now leaves the world and goes to the Father" (*John* 16:28). This return to the Father, the elevation "to the right hand of the Father," concretely realizes a messianic truth foretold in the Old Testament.

When the evangelist Mark tells us that "the Lord Jesus... was taken up into heaven" (*Mark* 16:19), his words echo the prophecy of the Lord recorded in *Psalm* 110:1: "The LORD said to my lord, 'Sit at my right hand, till I make your enemies your footstool.'" To sit at the right hand of God means to share in his kingly power and divine dignity. ❞

—Blessed John Paul II
12 April 1989

A SOUND CAME FROM HEAVEN LIKE THE RUSH OF A MIGHTY WIND

In the stained glass window depicting the third Glorious Mystery, the Holy Spirit appears in the form of a dove to extend heavenly rays of light on the apostles and the Blessed Virgin Mary. Tongues of fire appear on the heads of each of Jesus' followers who are gathered to pray.

Paragraph 1285 of the *Catechism of the Catholic Church* teaches that Confirmation is the sacrament through which baptized Christians are enriched with the strength of the Holy Spirit to become "more strictly obliged to spread and defend the faith by word and deed." Identify one way that you can, either by your words or by your actions, witness to your faith in the love of Jesus Christ. Ask the Holy Spirit to give you strength.

ACTS 2:1–4, 14–18

[1]When the day of Pentecost had come, they were all together in one place. [2]And suddenly a sound came from heaven like the rush of a mighty wind, and it filled all the house where they were sitting. [3]And there appeared to them tongues as of fire, distributed and resting on each one of them. [4]And they were all filled with the Holy Spirit and began to speak in other tongues, as the Spirit gave them utterance....

[14]But Peter, standing with the Eleven, lifted up his voice and addressed them, "Men of Judea and all who dwell in Jerusalem, let this be known to you, and give ear to my words. [15]For these men are not drunk as you suppose, since it is only the third hour of the day; [16]but this is what was spoken by the prophet Joel:

[17]And in the last days it shall be, God declares,
that I will pour out my Spirit upon all flesh,
and your sons and your daughters shall prophesy,
and your young men shall see visions,
and your old men shall dream dreams;
[18]yes, and on my menservants and my maidservants in those days
I will pour out my Spirit; and they shall prophesy."

1 Read *Acts* 1:13–14. How many people in the upper room became filled with the Holy Spirit? Why do you think that the Holy Spirit came to these people in a group instead of individually? Explain whether you think it was necessary that they be praying.

2 Read *Leviticus* 23:9–25. In the Old Testament, Pentecost was a harvest festival known as the feast of Weeks. Explain why the Israelites would not have been able to celebrate this religious festival until after they had entered the Promised Land.

3 The feast of Weeks specifically offered thanks for new grain. Read *John* 12:24–26. Explain how you think the New Testament Pentecost might be seen to fulfill Jesus' statement about grain.

4 Those who observe the apostles' behavior on Pentecost following the descent of the Holy Spirit assume that the apostles must have been drinking wine. What Old Testament figure also was assumed to have been drunk while praying (refer to *1 Samuel* 1:9–17 and *A Woman Sorely Troubled* on page 25)? What do you think this might suggest about the nature of the relationship between God and humanity that is fostered through intimate prayer?

PETER'S PRIMACY

Peter's primacy is apparent in this window, which places him front and center. He has adopted a Christ-like pose with his left arm outstretched holding the keys to the kingdom of heaven, while with his right hand he extends a blessing. His red robes identify him as an authority figure, emphasizing the role assigned to him by Jesus: "And I tell you, you are Peter, and on this rock I will build my Church, and the gates of Hades shall not prevail against it. I will give you the keys of the kingdom of heaven, and whatever you bind on earth shall be bound in heaven, and whatever you loose on earth shall be loosed in heaven" (*Matthew* 16:18–19).

Paragraph 881 of the *Catechism of the Catholic Church* teaches that the pastoral office of Peter is continued by the bishops under the primacy of the Pope, often called the chair of Peter. In the window, Peter is shown seated.

It is immediately after the descent of the Holy Spirit that Peter gives his first homily, opening with words from the prophet Joel: "And in the last days it shall be, God declares, that I will pour out my Spirit upon all flesh, and your sons and your daughters shall prophesy, and your young men shall see visions, and your old men shall dream dreams (*Acts* 2:17 and *Joel* 2:28 [*Joel* 3:1 NAB]). *Acts* 2:41 recounts that as a result of Peter's preaching that day, about 3,000 persons were baptized.

LOVE OF GOD

The Descent of the Holy Spirit is associated with love of God. It also is tied to the virtue of wisdom, one of the seven gifts of the Holy Spirit.

Jesus sums up the 10 Commandments into two great commandments—love of God and love of neighbor (*Matthew* 22:37–40). Love is the common denominator.

It requires wisdom for humanity to learn to love God. Paragraph 2658 of the *Catechism of the Catholic Church* teaches that it is only through love given by the Holy Spirit that Christians are able to pray: "'Hope does not disappoint us, because God's *love* has been poured into our hearts by the Holy Spirit who has been given to us.' ... Love is the source of prayer; whoever draws from it reaches the summit of prayer."

As you pray the third Glorious Mystery, ask Jesus to give you an increase in wisdom and to fill you more and more with his Spirit in order that you may in turn come to love God more and more.

Consider what your life might look like if you had more love for God. What things would you be doing differently? What is stopping you from making those changes right now?

An angel purifies Isaiah's lips with a burning coal.

THEN I SAID, 'HERE AM I! SEND ME'

The Old Testament window that parallels the Descent of the Holy Spirit shows Isaiah's lips being purified with fire by an angel. Isaiah is the first of the major prophets (with Jeremiah, Daniel, Baruch, and Ezekiel) whose writings constitute the lengthy prophetic books of the Old Testament. Following his apocalyptic vision of heaven, Isaiah immediately volunteers to go out and pronounce the word of the Lord.

This event foreshadows the tongues of fire that descend on the apostles, enabling them to go out and preach the good news of Jesus Christ.

Isaiah's prophecies include foretelling the birth of Immanuel to a virgin *(Isaiah* 7:14), announcing a shoot that would spring from the stump of Jesse *(Isaiah* 11:1), and foretelling the Messiah as the Lord's suffering servant *(Isaiah* 52:13—53:12).

ISAIAH 6:1—9

¹...I saw the Lord sitting upon a throne, high and lifted up; and his train filled the temple. ²Above him stood the seraphim; each had six wings: with two he covered his face, and with two he covered his feet, and with two he flew. ³And one called to another and said:

"Holy, holy, holy is the Lord of hosts;
the whole earth is full of his glory."

⁴And the foundations of the thresholds shook at the voice of him who called, and the house was filled with smoke. ⁵And I said: "Woe is me! For I am lost; for I am a man of unclean lips; for my eyes have seen the King, the Lord of hosts!"

⁶Then flew one of the seraphim to me, having in his hand a burning coal which he had taken with tongs from the altar. ⁷And he touched my mouth, and said: "Behold, this has touched your lips; your guilt is taken away, and your sin forgiven." ⁸And I heard the voice of the Lord saying, "Whom shall I send, and who will go for us?" Then I said, "Here am I! Send me."

⁹And he said, "Go, and say to this people:
'Hear and hear, but do not understand;
see and see, but do not perceive.'"

5 In *2 Kings* 2:11, Elijah is described as going up to heaven in a whirlwind. In *Acts* 2:2, the descent of the Holy Spirit from heaven is accompanied by a sound "like the rush of a mighty wind." Paragraph 691 of the *Catechism of the Catholic Church* teaches that "the term 'Spirit' translates the Hebrew word *ruah*, which, in its primary sense, means breath, air, wind." What is the relationship between breathing and speaking, and what do you think this implies about the relationship between the Holy Spirit as the breath of God, and Jesus Christ who is the Word of God? What do you think it implies about people who have been filled with the Holy Spirit?

6 Read *Isaiah* 6:1–4, which describes Isaiah's apocalyptic vision of God's Temple. What do you think that Isaiah was doing just before he was shown this vision? Based on the biblical text, where do you think that God's Temple is located?

7 In *Isaiah* 6:5, the prophet exclaims: "Woe is me! For I am lost; for I am a man of unclean lips; for my eyes have seen the King, the LORD of hosts!" What evidence is there in the biblical text that Isaiah has seen "the King, the LORD of hosts"? What do you think Isaiah fears is going to happen to him as a result (see *Exodus* 33:20)? Explain whether you feel that Isaiah's fear is justified.

8 There is considerable overlap in the Old Testament parallels for the first three Glorious Mysteries, apparent in repeated use of water, fire, and wind as symbols for the Holy Spirit. What purpose do you think is served by the tongues of fire that descend on those gathered for Pentecost? Explain whether you think that this is the same reason Isaiah's lips are touched with fire in *Isaiah* 6:6–8. What does Isaiah volunteer to do after his lips have been burned? How might this be related to the activities of the apostles after Pentecost?

9 In *Isaiah* 6:9, the voice of the LORD says to Isaiah: "Go, and say to this people: 'Hear and hear, but do not understand; see and see, but do not perceive.'" This is a common Old Testament theme, also appearing in *Psalm* 115:6, *Psalm* 135:17, and *Ezekiel* 12:2. Why do you think that God would go to the trouble to keep sending Old Testament prophets to people he knew were going to refuse to understand or perceive the LORD's words spoken through those prophets? What point do you think that God is trying to make?

10 Read *Luke* 7:20–23. In this passage, Jesus is responding to a question from John the Baptist. What essentially does John the Baptist want to know when he seeks to learn if Jesus is "he who is to come"? Jesus not only tells the messengers to report back to John the Baptist with what they have seen and heard, Jesus actually goes on to spell it out in very specific terms. Why do you think that Jesus does this? What is different about what Jesus tells the Baptist's messengers in the New Testament and what God tells his prophets in *Isaiah* 6:9 and elsewhere in the Old Testament?

> 66 Peter's [Pentecost] discourse testifies that with the Descent of the Holy Spirit the apostles definitively became aware of the vision of the kingdom that Christ had announced from the very beginning and of which he also had spoken after the Resurrection (*Acts* 1:3). Even then his hearers had asked him about the restoration of the kingdom of Israel (*Acts* 1:6), so deeply imbedded in their minds was the temporalistic interpretation of the messianic mission.
>
> Only after having received "the power" of the Spirit of truth, did they become "witnesses to Christ" and to his messianic kingdom, which was definitively brought into being when the glorified Christ "was seated at the right hand of the Father."
>
> In God's economy of salvation there is therefore a close connection between Christ's elevation and the descent of the Holy Spirit upon the apostles. From that moment the apostles became witnesses to the kingdom that will have no end. In this perspective the words that they heard after Christ's Ascension acquire a fullness of meaning, namely: "This Jesus who was taken up from you into heaven, will come in the same way as you saw him go into heaven" (*Acts* 1:11). This is a prophecy of a final and definitive fullness that will be had when, in the power of the Spirit of Christ, the whole divine plan in history will attain its fulfillment. 99
> —Blessed John Paul II
> 12 April 1989

I GO TO PREPARE A PLACE FOR YOU

The Assumption of the Blessed Virgin Mary was dogmatically defined by Pope Pius XII in *Munificentissimus Deus* (The Most Bountiful God) on November 1, 1950. Celebrated on August 15, Mary's Assumption is seen by the Church as a sign of the resurrection awaiting all Christians. Paragraph 966 of the *Catechism of the Catholic Church* teaches that the Assumption of the Blessed Virgin Mary "is a singular participation in her Son's Resurrection and an anticipation of the resurrection of other Christians."

In the Assumption Window, Mary stands amid angels and clouds of heaven with her gaze clearly focused on high.

What are some earthly situations threatening to pull your attention away from heavenly things? Explain whether you think it is possible for Christians to find a balance between dealing with valid earthly concerns and gazing at the things of heaven.

JOHN 14:1–11

[1]"Let not your hearts be troubled; believe in God, believe also in me. [2]In my Father's house are many rooms; if it were not so, would I have told you that I go to prepare a place for you? [3]And when I go and prepare a place for you, I will come again and will take you to myself that where I am you may be also. [4]And you know the way where I am going." [5]Thomas said to him, "Lord, we do not know where you are going; how can we know the way?" [6]Jesus said to him, "I am the way, and the truth, and the life; no one comes to the Father, but by me. [7]If you had known me, you would have known my Father also; henceforth you know him and have seen him."

[8]Philip said to him, "Lord, show us the Father, and we shall be satisfied." [9]Jesus said to him, "Have I been with you so long, and yet you do not know me, Philip? He who has seen me has seen the Father; how can you say, 'Show us the Father?' [10]Do you not believe that I am in the Father and the Father is in me? The words that I say to you I do not speak on my own authority; but the Father who dwells in me does his works. [11]Believe me that I am in the Father and the Father is in me; or else believe me for the sake of the works themselves."

1 In *John* 14:2, Jesus tells his followers that he is going away to prepare a place for them in his Father's house. What does Jesus indicate that he expects from his followers (see *John* 14:1)? Based on what you already know from Scripture, explain which of Jesus' followers you think may have come closest to meeting his expectations.

2 In *John* 14:5, Thomas expresses concern that the disciples do not know where Jesus is going. What has Jesus already said that makes this irrelevant in terms of following Jesus (see *John* 14:3)?

3 Upon which of the 10 Commandments does the Church base the obligation to participate in celebration of the Eucharist on Sundays and holy days (see *Exodus* 20:3–19)? What are the designated holy days of obligation (see *CCC* 2177)? Why do you think that the Church's liturgical calendar includes three Marian solemnities?

4 Paragraph 2185 of the *Catechism of the Catholic Church* teaches that in addition to participating in the Mass on Sundays and holy days, Catholics are encouraged to refrain from engaging in work or activities that hinder worship owed to God. What sort of difficulties might this impose on contemporary culture, and how do you think such difficulties might be overcome?

CONNECTION TO THE TEMPLE

In the Assumption Window a lily, symbol of spiritual purity, bursts into bloom above the pillars of the Temple at Mary's feet. As an image of the Church, the Blessed Virgin Mary also symbolizes the Temple of the Holy Spirit. Paragraph 797 of the *Catechism of the Catholic Church* establishes that the "Holy Spirit makes the Church 'the temple of the living God'," while paragraph 967 teaches that Mary "is the 'exemplary realization' (*typus*) of the Church."

St. John Chrysostom (347–407) urged Christians to embellish their "houses" with modesty and humility through prayer: "Make your dwelling place shine with the light of justice; adorn its walls with good works, like a lustre of pure gold, and replace walls and precious stones with faith and supernatural magnanimity, putting prayer above all other things." Those who devote themselves to prayer prepare a worthy dwelling (or Temple) for the Lord on earth.

In *John* 14:2–3, Jesus promises his disciples that he, in turn, goes to prepare a place in his Father's house in heaven for those who have been his devoted followers on earth.

The message is simple: Make room for God on earth, and God will make room for you in heaven. Christians' best example is seen in Mary's unselfish response to God at the Annunciation, which eventually leads to her glorious Assumption into heaven.

GRACE OF FINAL PERSEVERANCE

Grace of Final Perseverance is the fruit or virtue associated with the fourth Glorious Mystery.

The author of the *Letter to the Hebrews* encourages Christians to "...lay aside every weight, and sin which clings so closely, and let us run with perseverance the race that is set before us, looking to Jesus the pioneer and perfecter of our faith..." (*Hebrews* 12:1-2).

As the first and perfect disciple, the Blessed Virgin Mary ran the race of her earthly life filled with the grace of the Holy Spirit. From the time of her "Yes" to God at the Annunciation, to her flight into Egypt when King Herod sought to kill her Son, through the hidden years of life with Jesus and Joseph in Nazareth, to the painful days of Jesus' Passion and death on the cross, to clinging to hope until his Resurrection, the Blessed Virgin Mary teaches by her bold yet quiet example how to persevere to the end.

From heaven Mary continues to watch over all of her children with maternal love. As you meditate on the Mystery of Mary's Assumption, pray to receive the grace of final perseverance.

After decapitating Holofernes, Judith holds up his head.

STRUCK DOWN BY A WOMAN

The lower Assumption Window depicts an Old Testament scene in which Judith displays the head of Holofernes to the people of Israel who had been threatened by the Assyrian leader and his army.

Judith, who decapitated Holofernes with his own sword as he slept, risks her own life to spare the lives of her people. She is seen as a type of the Blessed Virgin Mary, whose cooperation with God's plan for the birth of Jesus was necessary to make possible the salvation of the world.

Judith is lauded for her efforts in words similar to those used to praise the Blessed Virgin Mary: "O daughter, you are blessed by the Most High God above all women on earth" and "May God grant this to be a perpetual honor to you."

JUDITH 13:15–20

15Then [Judith] took the head out of the bag and showed it to them, and said, "See, here is the head of Holofernes, the commander of the Assyrian army, and here is the canopy beneath which he lay in his drunken stupor. The Lord has struck him down by the hand of a woman. 16As the Lord lives, who has protected me in the way I went, it was my face that tricked him to his destruction, and yet he committed no act of sin with me, to defile and shame me."

17All the people were greatly astonished, and bowed down and worshiped God, and said with one accord, "Blessed are you, our God, who have brought into contempt this day the enemies of your people."

18And Uzziah said to her, "O daughter, you are blessed by the Most High God above all women on earth; and blessed be the Lord God, who created the heavens and the earth, who has guided you to strike the head of the leader of our enemies. 19Your hope will never depart from the hearts of men, as they remember the power of God. 20May God grant this to be a perpetual honor to you, and may he visit you with blessings, because you did not spare your own life when our nation was brought low, but have avenged our ruin, walking in the straight path before our God."

5 Read *Judith* 7:19–32. How long have the Israelites been surrounded by the Assyrians? What has caused the Israelites to lose courage and strength? How long does Uzziah suggest they hold out before surrendering? In *Judith* 7:30, what does Uzziah say that he hopes will happen in that amount of time?

6 Describe Judith's reputation among the Israelites (see *Judith* 8:1–8). How might her character figure in her decision to rebuke the elders? Why specifically is Judith upset (see *Judith* 8:9–16)?

7 Read *Judith* 8:17– 35. What alternative to surrender does Judith suggest to Uzziah? Why do you think that she refuses to tell him all of the details? Why do you think Uzziah accepts her idea?

8 Judith is recognized as an Old Testament type of Mary. Read *Judith* 9:1—13:20. Explain similarities and differences between Judith's campaign against the Assyrians and the way that the Blessed Virgin Mary fights to protect Christians. What does Judith have in common with the woman described in *Genesis* 3:15? *Eve*

9 Judith not only deceives Holofernes, she also murders him. Explain whether you think that Judith's actions are justified. Who does Judith credit with her success (see *Judith* 13:15)? Who does Judith believe protected her as she endeavored to defeat Holofernes and the Assyrians (see *Judith* 13:16)?

10 Why do you think Judith makes a point of mentioning that Holofernes committed no sin with her? Who does Uzziah believe was behind Judith's defeat of Holofernes (see *Judith* 13:18)?

ELEVATED ABOVE ALL WOMEN

The monogram at the top of the Assumption Window combines the first letters of the names Mary and Regina, a Latin name that means "Queen." This symbol is related to the Assumption of Mary because it explains the reason she is taken body and soul into heaven, and it also anticipates the next and final Glorious Mystery of the Rosary, the Coronation of Mary.

Height long has been associated with royal power. Kings and Queens always rule from "on high," never from "below." One result of the Blessed Virgin Mary's Assumption is that she becomes elevated above all women. She is exalted or raised up, and this is for the purpose of pointing the way to God. From her position in heaven, Mary is able to serve as the ultimate guide for Christians. She is a "great sign" in heaven (*Revelation* 12:1).

In an Old Testament parallel to the Assumption, Judith saves her people from destruction at the hand of an enemy and thus she becomes a type of the Blessed Virgin Mary, "blessed by the Most High God above all women on earth" (*Judith* 13:18).

" [The Blessed Virgin Mary] departed this world to return "to the Father's house" (*John* 14:2). And all this is not remote from us as it might seem at first sight, because all of us are children of the Father, God. All of us are brothers and sisters of Jesus, and all of us also are children of Mary, our Mother. All of us are journeying on toward this happiness we call heaven, which in reality is God.

And Mary helps us. She encourages us to ensure that every moment of our life is a step forward on this exodus, on this journey toward God. May she help us in this way to make the reality of heaven, God's greatness, also present in the life of our world. Is this not basically the paschal dynamism of the human being, of every person who wants to become heavenly, perfectly happy, by virtue of Christ's Resurrection?

The new Eve followed the new Adam in suffering and in the Passion, and so too in definitive joy. Christ is the first fruits, but his risen flesh is inseparable from that of his earthly Mother, Mary. In Mary all of humanity is involved in the Assumption to God—and together with her all of Creation, whose groans and sufferings, St. Paul tells us, are the birth pangs of the new humanity.

Thus are born the new heaven and the new earth in which death shall be no more, neither shall there be mourning nor crying nor pain any more (*Revelation* 21:1–4). "

—Pope Benedict XVI
15 August 2008

A WOMAN CLOTHED WITH THE SUN

The final Rosary Window, the Coronation of Mary, shows the Blessed Virgin being crowned in heaven. With his right hand, Jesus places the crown on his Mother's head. The Holy Spirit appears as a dove overhead.

In his encyclical *Spe Salvi* (Christian Hope), Pope Benedict XVI describes the Blessed Virgin Mary as a star of hope: "On our common voyage on the ocean of history we need 'lights of hope,' people who draw light from Christ and who thus offer light for our passage. Who better than Mary can be for us a star of hope?"

At the top of the window the hand of God extends from a cloud, denoting the mysterious nature of Divine Providence.

Would you feel hopeful or apprehensive if you learned that God intended to take a more active role in your life? What do you think that men and women can do to more readily recognize God's presence in their everyday lives?

REVELATION 11:19–12:6

[19]Then God's temple in heaven was opened, and the ark of his covenant was seen within his temple; and there were flashes of lightning, loud noises, peals of thunder, an earthquake, and heavy hail.

[1]And a great sign appeared in heaven, a woman clothed with the sun, with the moon under her feet, and on her head a crown of twelve stars; [2]she was with child and she cried out in her pangs of birth, in anguish for delivery. [3]And another sign appeared in heaven; behold, a great red dragon, with seven heads and ten horns, and seven diadems upon his heads. [4]His tail swept down a third of the stars of heaven, and cast them to the earth. And the dragon stood before the woman who was about to bear a child, that he might devour her child when she brought it forth; [5]she brought forth a male child, one who is to rule all the nations with a rod of iron, but her child was caught up to God and to his throne, [6]and the woman fled into the wilderness, where she has a place prepared by God, in which to be nourished for one thousand two hundred and sixty days.

1 In ancient cultures, the role of the Queen Mother was well established as second in power only to the king. What practical considerations might have led to the development of this practice (see *1 Kings* 11:1–3 and *1 Chronicles* 3:1–9)? Read *1 Kings* 1:1–31. What is the reaction of Solomon's mother, Bathsheba, when she learns that Adonijah has appointed himself to reign as king after David?

2 Read *1 Kings* 2:13–25. What do you think motivates Bathsheba into agreeing to speak to Solomon on behalf of Adonijah? What does the manner in which Solomon receives his mother disclose about his respect for her judgment? Why do you think that Solomon then acts in complete contradiction to what his mother asks of him?

3 What does the story of Solomon and his mother suggest about the reasons Christ the King might have chosen to crown his Mother Queen of Heaven? Explain whether you think that the Blessed Virgin Mary functions a figurehead Queen of Heaven or whether she rules with actual authority.

4 The book of *Revelation* describes an apocalyptic vision of heaven following Jesus' Ascension. Read *Revelation* 11:19—12:1. What is the "great sign" that appears immediately after God's Temple in heaven is opened? What about this sign suggests royalty?

CROWNED IN GLORY

In the Coronation Window, Jesus and the Blessed Virgin Mary appear wearing golden crowns. Jesus is shown using his right hand to bestow royal honor, blessing, and authority upon his Mother.

Pope Pius XII instituted the feast of the Queenship of Mary in 1954. Devotion to the Blessed Virgin Mary as the sovereign Mother of heaven and earth is celebrated on August 22. A scriptural portrait of the Queen of Heaven appears in *Revelation* 12:1, where she is described as "a woman clothed with the sun, with the moon under her feet, and on her head a crown of twelve stars."

The most distinguishing characteristic of the woman clothed with the sun is neither her crown nor her glorious attire. It is the fact that she is pregnant. Mary's motherhood is of utmost importance because it is she who gives birth to the Savior of the world.

Paragraph 972 of the *Catechism of the Catholic Church* teaches that the Blessed Virgin Mary is the eschatological icon of the Church: "[T]he Mother of Jesus, in the glory which she possesses in body and soul in heaven, is the image and beginning of the Church as it is to be perfected in the world to come. Likewise she shines forth on earth, until the day of the Lord shall come, a sign of certain hope and comfort to the pilgrim People of God."

FRUITS OF PRAYER

DEVOTION TO MARY

The virtue associated with the fifth Glorious Mystery, the Coronation of the Blessed Virgin, is devotion to Mary. This Mystery also fittingly is associated with eternal happiness.

In his *Second Letter to Timothy*, St. Paul writes about the happiness awaiting Christians: "I have fought the good fight, I have finished the race, I have kept the faith. From now on there is laid up for me the crown of righteousness, which the Lord, the righteous judge, will award to me on that Day, and not only to me but also to all who have loved his appearing" (*2 Timothy* 4:7–8).

Who serves as a better example of having "fought the good fight" and "kept the faith" than the Blessed Virgin Mary? The Church teaches that after her death, Mary was taken up into heaven body and soul, where she was "exalted by the Lord as Queen over all things" (*CCC* 966).

Throughout history, countless men and women have displayed their devotion to the Virgin Mary as Queen of Heaven and Queen of their hearts. What are some ways that you can show your devotion to the Blessed Virgin Mary and her Son, Jesus Christ?

Queen Esther kneels in homage before King Ahasuerus.

THE KING HELD OUT THE GOLDEN SCEPTER

The Old Testament parallel to the Coronation of Mary depicts Esther kneeling before King Ahasuerus. Like Judith, Esther also took action to rescue her people when they were threatened with death.

Esther was Jewish, but her guardian Mordecai kept her background a secret. When the king's second-in-command, Haman, plotted to kill all the Jews in the kingdom, Mordecai entreated Esther to speak to the king. Turning to God, Esther was able to vanquish her enemy through mortification, fasting, and prayer. The Church traditionally sees in her the personification of noble virtues.

The king responds favorably to Esther's entreaties, nullifying the order to kill the Jews. The treacherous Haman meets his death instead.

ESTHER 8:3–8

[3]Then Esther spoke again to the king; she fell at his feet and besought him with tears to avert the evil design of Haman the Agagite and the plot which he had devised against the Jews. [4]And the king held out the golden scepter to Esther, [5]and Esther rose and stood before the king. And she said, "If it please the king, and if I have found favor in his sight, and if the thing seem right before the king, and I be pleasing in his eyes, let an order be written to revoke the letters devised by Haman the Agagite, the son of Hammedatha, which he wrote to destroy the Jews who are in all the provinces of the king. [6]For how can I endure to see the calamity that is coming to my people? Or how can I endure to see the destruction of my kindred?" [7]Then King Ahasuerus said to Queen Esther and to Mordecai the Jew, "Behold, I have given Esther the house of Haman, and they have hanged him on the gallows, because he would lay hands on the Jews. [8]And you may write as you please with regard to the Jews, in the name of the king, and seal it with the king's ring; for an edict written in the name of the king and sealed with the king's ring cannot be revoked."

5 The purpose of a sign is to point people toward something. To what do you think the "great sign" in *Revelation* 12:1 is pointing? Explain whether you think that this is a fitting task for royalty. What do you think that the 12 stars crowning the woman represent?

6 In *Revelation* 12:2, the most significant detail about the "woman clothed with the sun" is that she is pregnant. Who do you think is represented by the dragon waiting to devour her child? The child's destiny is described in *Revelation* 12:5. What clue does this provide about the identity of the child and his Father (see *Psalm* 2:7–9)?

7 Read *Esther* 1:1—8:8 (chapters 13—15 will be interspersed in this section of the RSV translation, and chapters B–D will be interspersed in the NAB translation). How does Esther originally come to be appointed queen by King Ahasuerus? What does Mordecai the Jew do to offend the king's second-in-command, Haman?

8 In his anger over Mordecai's behavior, what punishment does Haman plot against all of the Jews in the land? How is it that King Ahasuerus does not know that Esther is a Jew?

9 Read Esther's prayer, which can be found at *Esther* 14:1–19 in the RSV and at *Esther* C:12–30 in the NAB. What does Esther do before she approaches God in prayer? What does the fact that Esther's non-Jewish maidservants join in her prayer imply about Esther's character? What does Esther say the Jews have done that has put them into the hands of their enemies?

10 How does Esther's behavior in saving her people resemble the way that Mary is involved in the salvation of humanity?

Sal•ve Re•gi•na Hail, Holy Queen

The **Salve Regina,** composed during the Middle Ages, is one of the concluding prayers of the Rosary. The Latin **Salve Regina** also traditionally is sung to conclude nightly Liturgy of the Hours prayers between the seasons of Easter and Advent. The English translation can be found on the back flap of the cover of this book.

Salve, Regina, Mater misericordiæ,
vita, dulcedo, et spes nostra, salve.
ad te clamamus exsules filii Hevæ,
ad te suspiramus, gementes et flentes
in hac lacrimarum valle.
Eia, ergo, advocata nostra, illos tuos
misericordes oculos ad nos converte;
et Iesum, benedictum fructum ventris tui,
nobis post hoc exsilium ostende.
O clemens, O pia, O dulcis Virgo Maria.

" The books of *Tobit, Judith,* and *Esther,* although dealing with the history of the chosen people, have the character of allegorical and moral narrative….[*Dei Verbum*] points out the principal purpose of the plan of salvation in the Old Testament is "to prepare for the coming of Christ, the redeemer of all, and of the messianic kingdom, to announce this coming by prophecy" (*Luke* 24:44, *John* 5:39, and *1 Peter* 1:10) and to indicate its meaning through various types (*1 Corinthians* 10:11).

Dei Verbum teaches that books of the Old Testament, in accordance with the state of humanity before Christ, "reveal to all men the knowledge of God and of man and the ways in which God, just and merciful, deals with men. These books, though they also contain some things that are incomplete and temporary, nevertheless show us true divine pedagogy." They give expression to a "lively sense of God," "sound wisdom about human life," and "a wonderful treasury of prayers in which is present in a hidden way the mystery of our salvation."

The Old Testament must be received by Christians with devotion….This doctrine enables us to take a further step in determining the significance of our faith. "To believe in a Christian way" means to attain, according to the spirit that we have spoken about, the light of divine revelation from the books of the Old Covenant as well. "
—Blessed John Paul II
8 May 1985

HE SAW THE SPIRIT OF GOD DESCENDING LIKE A DOVE

The stained glass windows that depict the Creed and original 15 Mysteries of the Rosary were installed at St. Augustin Catholic Church in Des Moines, Iowa, in 1935. The artist Charles Connick died in 1945, more than 50 years before Blessed John Paul II introduced the Luminous Mysteries of the Rosary, so there are no matching stained glass windows depicting those New Testament events and their corresponding Old Testament parallels.

Most visual representations of Jesus' baptism in the Jordan River, however, include the Spirit of God descending like a dove, a detail emphasized in all four Gospels. Read *Matthew* 3:16–17, *Mark* 1:9–11, *Luke* 3:21–22, and *John* 1:32–34. Besides the dove, what other detail do all four of the Gospel writers include about the relationship between Jesus and God?

Paragraph 1270 of the *Catechism of the Catholic Church* teaches that in the sacrament of Baptism, Christians are reborn as children of God and must "participate in the apostolic and missionary activity of the People of God." Describe one apostolate or missionary activity that interests you.

MATTHEW 3:1–17

¹In those days came John the Baptist, preaching in the wilderness of Judea, ²"Repent, for the kingdom of heaven is at hand." ³For this is he who was spoken of by the prophet Isaiah when he said,

"The voice of one crying in the wilderness:
Prepare the way of the Lord,
make his paths straight."

⁴Now John wore a garment of camel's hair, and a leather belt around his waist; and his food was locusts and wild honey. ⁵Then went out to him Jerusalem and all Judea and all the region about the Jordan, ⁶and they were baptized by him in the river Jordan, confessing their sins.

⁷But when he saw many of the Pharisees and Sadducees coming for baptism, he said to them, "You brood of vipers! Who warned you to flee from the wrath to come? ⁸Bear fruit that befits repentance, ⁹and do not presume to say to yourselves, 'We have Abraham as our father'; for I tell you, God is able from these stones to raise up children to Abraham. ¹⁰Even now the axe is laid to the root of the trees; every tree therefore that does not bear good fruit is cut down and thrown into the fire.

¹¹"I baptize you with water for repentance, but he who is coming after me is mightier than I, whose sandals I am not worthy to carry; he will baptize you with the Holy Spirit and with fire. ¹²His winnowing fork is in his hand, and he will clear his threshing floor and gather his wheat into the granary, but the chaff he will burn with unquenchable fire."

¹³Then Jesus came from Galilee to the Jordan to John, to be baptized by him. ¹⁴John would have prevented him, saying, "I need to be baptized by you, and do you come to me?" ¹⁵But Jesus answered him, "Let it be so now; for thus it is fitting for us to fulfil all righteousness." Then he consented. ¹⁶And when Jesus was baptized, he went up immediately from the water, and behold, the heavens were opened and he saw the Spirit of God descending like a dove, and alighting on him; ¹⁷and behold, a voice from heaven, saying, "This is my beloved Son, with whom I am well pleased."

[handwritten: In the desert prepare the way of the Lord. Make straight in the wasteland a highway for our God]

1 All four of the Gospel writers focus on John's definition of himself as a voice crying in the wilderness in order to prepare the way of the Lord (see *Matthew* 3:3, *Mark* 1:2–4, *Luke* 3:2–6, and *John* 1:19–23). John's name "the Baptist" further identifies his role. Explain why the image of the voice from *Isaiah* 40:3 might be considered fitting for the person who would baptize Jesus.

2 In *Luke* 3:3, John's baptism is referred to as "a baptism of repentance for the forgiveness of sins." With what is it associated in *Matthew* 3:5–6? How might these associations help John the Baptist to "prepare the way of the Lord"? What do you think is meant by "way of the Lord," and why might some preparation be needed?

[handwritten: acknowledge sins]

3 Read *Genesis* 6:5—8:12, which records the account of Noah and the Flood. Paragraph 1219 of the *Catechism of the Catholic Church* teaches that the Church sees in Noah's ark "a prefiguring of salvation by Baptism." What aspect of the sacrament of Baptism do you think that the ark represents? What do you think is represented by the Flood waters? Who do you think that Noah represents?

JESUS CAME TO BE BAPTIZED

Because Jesus is sinless, it is normal to ask for what purpose he undergoes baptism in the Jordan. While Jesus is like men and women in all things but sin (*Hebrews* 4:15), John the Baptist differentiates between the nature of the baptism that he performs and sacramental Baptism: "[H]e who sent me to baptize with water said to me, 'He on whom you see the Spirit descend and remain, this is he who baptizes with the Holy Spirit'" (*John* 1:33).

Paragraph 720 of the *Catechism of the Catholic Church* teaches: "[B]aptism in water and the Spirit will be a new birth," and this statement provides a powerful clue about what is going on with Jesus' baptism by John. In the biblical account of the Flood (*Genesis* 6:5—8:12), water is associated with death. One man, Noah, is found to be good, so God chooses to save all that is good in the ark. The 40 days of rain represent God opening the heavens and allowing water to fall, returning the earth to the watery void that existed before Creation (*Genesis* 1:1–2).

Jesus, who is sinless, symbolizes all that is good about humanity. He enters into the waters and is baptized in order to provide safe passage for others. Through the sacrament of Baptism, men and women enter into the body of Christ, pass safely through the waters of death, and are reborn. Jesus acts as the ark, an image of the Church. Christians are protected from death and experience safety and salvation when they become part of the body of Christ. Whatever is not good in humanity—sin—is destroyed.

OPENNESS TO THE HOLY SPIRIT

The fruit associated with the first Luminous Mystery is openness to the Holy Spirit. Paragraph 1831 of the *Catechism of the Catholic Church* teaches that the gifts of the Holy Spirit—wisdom, understanding, counsel, fortitude, knowledge, piety, and fear of the Lord—are received in Baptism and strengthened at Confirmation in order to "make the faithful docile in readily obeying divine inspirations." Docile means open to the Spirit and easily taught. Christians who are open to the Spirit are attentive and available, ready to go where directed.

The Prayer to the Holy Spirit is a fitting introduction to meditation on the Baptism of Jesus:
Come Holy Spirit, fill the
 hearts of your faithful
 and kindle in them the
 fire of your love.
Send forth your Spirit, and
 they shall be created,
 and you shall renew the
 face of the earth.
O, God, who by the light
 of the Holy Spirit did
 instruct the hearts of
 the faithful, grant that
 by the same Holy Spirit
 we may be truly wise
 and ever rejoice in his
 consolation, through
 Christ our Lord.

EXODUS 14:5–29

[5]When the king of Egypt was told that the people had fled, the mind of Pharaoh and his servants was changed toward the people, and they said, "What is this we have done, that we have let Israel go from serving us?" [6]So he made ready his chariot and took his army with him, [7]and took six hundred picked chariots and all the other chariots of Egypt with officers over all of them. [8]And the LORD hardened the heart of Pharaoh king of Egypt and he pursued the sons of Israel as they went forth defiantly. [9]The Egyptians pursued them, Pharaoh's horses and chariots and his horsemen and his army, and overtook them encamped at the sea, by Pihahiroth, in front of Baalzephon.

[10]When Pharaoh drew near, the sons of Israel lifted up their eyes, and behold, the Egyptians were marching after them; and they were in great fear. And the sons of Israel cried out to the LORD; [11]and they said to Moses, "Is it because there are no graves in Egypt that you have taken us away to die in the wilderness? What have you done to us, in bringing us out of Egypt? [12]Is not this what we said to you in Egypt, 'Let us alone and let us serve the Egyptians'? For it would have been better for us to serve the Egyptians than to die in the wilderness." [13]And Moses said to the people, "Fear not, stand firm, and see the salvation of the LORD, which he will work for you today; for the Egyptians whom you see today you shall never see again. [14]The LORD will fight for you, and you have only to be still." [15]The LORD said to Moses, "Why do you cry to me? Tell the sons of Israel to go forward. [16]Lift up your rod, and stretch out your hand over the sea and divide it, that the sons of Israel may go on dry ground through the sea. [17]And I will harden the hearts of the Egyptians so that they shall go in after them, and I will get glory over Pharaoh and all his host, his chariots, and his horsemen. [18]And the Egyptians shall know that I am the LORD, when I have gotten glory over Pharaoh, his chariots, and his horsemen."

[19]Then the angel of God who went before the host of Israel moved and went behind them; and the pillar of cloud moved from before them and stood behind them, [20]coming between the host of Egypt and the host of Israel. And there was the cloud and the darkness; and the night passed without one coming near the other all night.

[21]Then Moses stretched out his hand over the sea; and the LORD drove the sea back by a strong east wind all night, and made the sea dry land, and the waters were divided. [22]And the sons of Israel went into the midst of the sea on dry ground, the waters being a wall to them on their right hand and on their left. [23]The Egyptians pursued, and went in after them into the midst of the sea, all Pharaoh's horses, his chariots, and his horsemen. [24]And in the morning watch the LORD in the pillar of fire and cloud looked down upon the host of the Egyptians, and discomfited the host of the Egyptians, [25]clogging their chariot wheels so that they drove heavily; and the Egyptians said, "Let us flee from before Israel; for the LORD fights for them against the Egyptians."

[26]Then the LORD said to Moses, "Stretch out your hand over the sea, that the water may come back upon the Egyptians, upon their chariots, and upon their horsemen." [27]So Moses stretched forth his hand over the sea, and the sea returned to its usual flow when the morning appeared; and the Egyptians fled into it, and the LORD routed the Egyptians in the midst of the sea. [28]The waters returned and covered the chariots and the horsemen and all the host of Pharaoh that had followed them into the sea; not so much as one of them remained. [29]But the sons of Israel walked on dry ground through the sea, the waters being a wall to them on their right hand and on their left.

Faith w/out works is dead

4 Compare the dove's role in the account of the Flood (see *Genesis* 8:1–12) with its role in the account of Jesus' baptism (see *Matthew* 3:16–17). Explain how the dove can be seen as a suitable image for the action of the Holy Spirit in Baptism (see *CCC* 701).

5 Read the account of the Israelites' passage through the Red Sea in *Exodus* 14:5–29. How does this account resemble the account of Noah and the Flood found in *Genesis* 6:5—8:12? In what ways do the two events differ?

6 In the account of the Israelites' passage through the Red Sea, what aspect of the sacrament of Baptism do you think that the sea represents? Who or what is responsible for the Israelites receiving safe passage through the water? – *God* *Moses*

7 In *Exodus* 14:10–14, what is the Israelites' attitude when they learn that Pharaoh and his army have pursued them as they left Egypt? What is Moses' advice to the Israelites?

8 In *Exodus* 14:15–18, what point do you think that the LORD is trying to make when he asks Moses: "Why do you cry to me?" For what purpose does Moses say that the LORD intends to fight for the Israelites against Pharaoh and the Egyptians?

9 In *Exodus* 14:19–21, how does God prevent the Egyptians from slaughtering the Israelites during the night before the Israelites enter the Red Sea? How does God then go about giving the Israelites safe passage through the Red Sea? What do you think possesses the Egyptians to rush headlong into the sea after the Israelites? In *Exodus* 14:24–29, what conclusion do the Egyptians reach about the God of the Israelites? What specific things does the LORD do to arrange for the Egyptians' defeat?

10 Explain what is sanctified in Jesus' baptism in the Jordan, and how that event makes it possible for a Christian to die with Jesus Christ in the sacrament of his or her own Baptism (see *CCC* 536). Read the *Letter to the Romans* 6:3–11. What does St. Paul teach is the ultimate benefit of being baptized into Christ Jesus?

> **"** At the Jordan Jesus reveals himself with an extraordinary humility, reminiscent of the poverty and simplicity of the child laid in the manger, and he anticipates the sentiments with which, at the end of his days on earth, he will come to the point of washing the feet of the disciples and suffering the terrible humiliation of the cross.
>
> The Son of God, the one who is without sin, puts himself among sinners, and demonstrates God's closeness to the process of the human being's conversion. Jesus takes upon his shoulders the burden of sin of the whole of humanity. He begins his mission by putting himself in our place, in the place of sinners, in the perspective of the cross.
>
> While absorbed in prayer Jesus emerges from the water after his baptism. At that moment, "the heaven was opened, and the Holy Spirit descended upon him in bodily form as a dove" (*Luke* 3:21-22), and words were heard that had never been heard before: "You are my beloved Son; with you I am well pleased" (*Luke* 3:22). **"**
> —Pope Benedict XVI
> 10 January 2010

THE SONS OF ISRAEL WENT INTO THE MIDST OF THE SEA

There are a number of Old Testament passages that could serve as a parallel to Jesus' baptism in the Jordan River, including Noah and the Flood (*Genesis* 6:5—8:12) and Joshua leading the Israelites across the Jordan River into the Promised Land (*Joshua* 3:1–17). The account of the Israelites walking on dry ground through the sea, however, is a mandatory reading at the Easter Vigil, the time when adult catechumens are baptized into the Church, and it is singled out as an Old Testament prefiguration of Baptism in paragraph 1221 of the *Catechism of the Catholic Church*: "But above all, the crossing of the Red Sea, literally the liberation of Israel from slavery in Egypt, announces the liberation wrought by Baptism." Old Testament parallels to all the Luminous Mysteries in this Bible study are taken from *Exodus*.

YOU HAVE KEPT THE GOOD WINE UNTIL NOW

At the wedding at Cana, the Blessed Virgin Mary demonstrates her effectiveness as an intercessor. In *Treatise on True Devotion to the Blessed Virgin*, St. Louis de Montfort observes that "the greatest saints, those richest in grace and virtue, will be the most assiduous in praying to the most Blessed Virgin, looking up to her as the perfect model to imitate and as a powerful helper to assist them." When was the last time that you asked Mary to intercede with a problem? What situation in your life do you think might benefit from her intercession right now? Pray for her assistance.

JOHN 2:1–11

¹On the third day there was a marriage at Cana in Galilee, and the mother of Jesus was there; ²Jesus also was invited to the marriage, with his disciples. ³When the wine failed, the mother of Jesus said to him, "They have no wine." ⁴And Jesus said to her, "O woman, what have you to do with me? My hour has not yet come." ⁵His mother said to the servants, "Do whatever he tells you." ⁶Now six stone jars were standing there, for the Jewish rites of purification, each holding twenty or thirty gallons. ⁷Jesus said to them, "Fill the jars with water." And they filled them up to the brim. ⁸He said to them, "Now draw some out, and take it to the steward of the feast." So they took it. ⁹When the steward of the feast tasted the water now become wine, and did not know where it came from (though the servants who had drawn the water knew), the steward of the feast called the bridegroom ¹⁰and said to him, "Every man serves the good wine first; and when men have drunk freely, then the poor wine; but you have kept the good wine until now." ¹¹This, the first of his signs, Jesus did at Cana in Galilee, and manifested his glory; and his disciples believed in him.

1 In *John* 2:1–11, what problem do the newlyweds face? What does Jesus say in response when the Blessed Virgin Mary brings this problem to his attention? In *John* 2:4, Jesus appears inclined to ignore his Mother's request. What excuse does Jesus use, and do you think that this is a valid reason for him not to get involved?

2 How do Mary's instructions to the servants indicate that she expects Jesus to solve the newlyweds' problem? Explain whether you think that Jesus intends to solve this problem all along. What does Jesus ask the servants to do? Does this seem like a reasonable request? Why do you think that the servants so readily comply?

3 For what purpose were the six stone jars usually used? If each jar holds 20 to 30 gallons, how much liquid would all six jars hold? What are some possible reasons that might explain why Jesus chose to solve the newlyweds' problem in such a generous fashion?

signs miracles

John's Gospel presents **signs** instead of miracles. In addition to providing evidence of supernatural power—that is, manifesting Jesus' glory and proving that he is indeed the Messiah—the **signs** in *John's Gospel* point forward to something more. The **sign** at the wedding in Cana points ahead to the Eucharist as well as to the Church as the bride of Christ.

4 Explain how the sign of Jesus turning water into wine at the wedding in Cana foreshadows the sacrament of the Eucharist.

5 In *Mark* 14:25, at the institution of the Eucharist, Jesus tells his disciples: "Truly, I say to you, I shall not drink again of the fruit of the vine until that day when I drink it new in the kingdom of God." The sign of the water turned to wine takes place at a wedding. Paragraph 1335 of the *Catechism of the Catholic Church* teaches that this sign "makes manifest the fulfillment of the wedding feast in the Father's kingdom, where the faithful will drink the new wine that has become the blood of Christ." In *John's Gospel,* who does John the Baptist identify as a bridegroom (see *John* 3:28–29)? In the book of *Revelation*, who is identified as the bridegroom (see *Revelation* 19:7)? Explain whether you think these are the same person. Who does *Revelation* identify as the bride (see *Revelation* 21:2)?

EVIDENCE OF EMMANUEL

Jesus' transformation of water into wine at the wedding in Cana (*John* 2:1–11) is the first of the signs he performs in the *Fourth Gospel*. The words of the Blessed Virgin Mary to the servants— "Do whatever he tells you" (*John* 2:5)—are widely understood as instructions that are applicable to Jesus' followers in every age.

This account of an intimate interaction between Jesus and Mary mystifies some readers, who are perplexed at Jesus' apparent indifference to his Mother's request. It is clear from Mary's instructions to the servants, however, that she does not interpret Jesus' response as disrespectful or as a denial.

Mary and Jesus relate not only as creature and Creator (in which Mary respects Jesus' divine nature), but also as Mother and Son (in which Jesus shows proper filial respect for the woman through whom he has received his human nature). When Jesus calls his Mother "woman," he is acknowledging that in this situation they are communicating on a human level and that the sign he is about to perform is done at her request.

By complying with his Mother's request, Jesus sets in motion events that will make salvation possible for all humanity.

The six stone jars represent the framework Jesus will use for re-Creation. They first contain an inadequate filling of water (a substance also present in *Genesis* 1:1–2 at the beginning of Creation). In order to celebrate the fulfillment of the wedding— and the union of human and divine in the second person of the Blessed Trinity—the water must become wine. With this sign, Jesus indicates what will be accomplished in the marriage of the human and the divine, and he provides evidence that he is indeed "Emmanuel (which means, God with us)" (*Matthew* 1:23).

FRUITS OF PRAYER

TRUST IN MARY'S INTERCESSION

Paragraph 2618 of the *Catechism of the Catholic Church* explains that the account of the wedding at Cana "reveals to us how Mary prays and intercedes in faith." The newlyweds had a problem, which Mary took to Jesus. She interceded, and he solved the problem. When meditating on the second Luminous Mystery, Christians pray for the virtue of being able to trust in Mary's intercession.

Have you ever asked another Christian to pray for you? What about that person's faith prompted you to ask them to intercede for you? Mary's faith and her role as Mother of the Church make her a perfect intercessor.

The Memorare:
Remember, O most
    gracious Virgin Mary,
    never was it known
    that anyone who fled
    to thy protection,
    implored thy help, or
    sought thy intercession
    was left unaided.
Inspired by this confidence,
    I fly unto thee, O Virgin
    of virgins, my Mother;
    to thee do I come,
    before thee I stand,
    sinful and sorrowful.
O Mother of the Word
    Incarnate, despise not
    my petitions,
    but in thy mercy hear
    and answer me.

EXODUS 17:1–7

¹All the congregation of the sons of Israel moved on from the wilderness of Sin by stages, according to the commandment of the LORD, and camped at Rephidim; but there was no water for the people to drink. ²Therefore the people found fault with Moses, and said, "Give us water to drink." And Moses said to them, "Why do you find fault with me? Why do you put the LORD to the test?" ³But the people thirsted there for water, and the people murmured against Moses, and said, "Why did you bring us up out of Egypt, to kill us and our children and our cattle with thirst?" ⁴So Moses cried to the LORD, "What shall I do with this people? They are almost ready to stone me." ⁵And the LORD said to Moses, "Pass on before the people, taking with you some of the elders of Israel; and take in your hand the rod with which you struck the Nile, and go. ⁶Behold, I will stand before you there on the rock at Horeb, and you shall strike the rock, and water shall come out of it, that the people may drink." And Moses did so, in the sight of the elders of Israel. ⁷And he called the name of the place Massah and Meribah, because of the fault-finding of the sons of Israel, and because they put the LORD to the test by saying, "Is the LORD among us or not?"

6 Read *Exodus* 17:1–7. What problem do the Israelites face? Compare it with the problem faced by the newlyweds in Cana (see *John* 2:1–11). Explain which problem you think is more severe.

7 How does the LORD go about solving the Israelites' problem? Why do you think that God has Moses use the same rod that was used in the plagues against Egypt? What happened to the Nile when Moses struck it (see *Exodus* 7:14–21)? In *Exodus* 17:6, what happens to the rock in the wilderness when Moses strikes it?

8 In *Exodus* 17:7, what question about the LORD do the Israelites want answered? Do you think that God gives them a sufficient answer? Explain whether you think water from the rock is a suitable parallel for the Mystery associated with the wedding at Cana.

9 Read the *First Letter to the Corinthians* 10:1–4, in which St. Paul describes water from the Rock as "supernatural drink." What was the "supernatural food" he writes that all of the Israelites ate while journeying in the wilderness? What radical interpretation does St. Paul express about the nature of the Rock? Explain how the water from this Rock foreshadows the sacrament of Eucharist.

10 Read *Psalm* 95. In the first verse, to what is God compared? What is the Psalmist encouraging people to do, and why do you think that he is relying on the account about water from the Rock? How does the Psalmist describe God's feelings about what happened at Meribah and Massah? What are the consequences to the descendants of the Israelites as a result of their ancestors' behavior in the wilderness?

AND THE ROCK WAS CHRIST

An intriguing detail about the Israelites' time in the wilderness concerns the water that flowed from the rock (*Exodus* 17:1–7). St. Paul expresses the radical idea that this Rock at Massah and Meribah was Jesus: "[O]ur fathers…all drank the same supernatural drink. For they drank from the supernatural Rock which followed them, and the Rock was Christ" (*1 Corinthians* 10:1–4).

If Jesus is the source of this supernatural drink, then this Old Testament event is a fitting parallel to the second Luminous Mystery, the sign of water being turned into wine. It is significant that the Israelites had been testing God and asking: "Is the LORD among us or not?" (*Exodus* 17:7). Scripture implies that God was indeed with them—and God also was at the wedding in Cana.

BLESSED ARE THE POOR IN SPIRIT, FOR THEIRS IS THE KINGDOM OF HEAVEN

In *Matthew* 5:1–20, Jesus proclaims the kingdom of heaven and explains how it operates, and he goes out of his way to establish that he has no intention of abolishing the law and the prophets of the Old Testament. The giving of the Law on Mt. Sinai (*Exodus* 19:16—20:20) often is seen as a foreshadowing of Jesus' New Testament Sermon on the Mount, which includes not only the Beatitudes but also the prayer known as The Lord's Prayer, or the Our Father (*Matthew* 6:8–13).

The word beatitude means blessing, and each begins "Blessed are …." This sometimes is translated from the original Greek as "Happy are …." Write three beatitudes of your own describing occasions of happiness you have experienced as a result of engaging in specific virtuous practices.

MATTHEW 5:1–20

¹Seeing the crowds, he went up on the mountain, and when he sat down his disciples came to him. ²And he opened his mouth and taught them, saying:

³"Blessed are the poor in spirit, for theirs is the kingdom of heaven.

⁴"Blessed are those who mourn, for they shall be comforted.

⁵"Blessed are the meek, for they shall inherit the earth. *Kingdom*

⁶"Blessed are those who hunger and thirst for righteousness, for they shall be satisfied.

⁷"Blessed are the merciful, for they shall obtain mercy.

⁸"Blessed are the pure in heart, for they shall see God.

⁹"Blessed are the peacemakers, for they shall be called sons of God.

¹⁰"Blessed are those who are persecuted for righteousness' sake, for theirs is the kingdom of heaven.

¹¹"Blessed are you when men revile you and persecute you and utter all kinds of evil against you falsely on my account. ¹²Rejoice and be glad, for your reward is great in heaven, for so men persecuted the prophets who were before you.

¹³"You are the salt of the earth; but if salt has lost its taste, how shall its saltiness be restored? It is no longer good for anything except to be thrown out and trodden under foot by men.

¹⁴"You are the light of the world. A city set on a hill cannot be hidden. ¹⁵Nor do men light a lamp and put it under a bushel, but on a stand, and it gives light to all in the house. ¹⁶Let your light so shine before men, that they may see your good works and give glory to your Father who is in heaven.

¹⁷"Do not think that I have come to abolish the law and the prophets; I have come not to abolish them but to fulfil them. ¹⁸For truly, I say to you, till heaven and earth pass away, not an iota, not a dot, will pass from the law until all is accomplished. ¹⁹Whoever then relaxes one of the least of these commandments and teaches men so, shall be called least in the kingdom of heaven; but he who does them and teaches them shall be called great in the kingdom of heaven. ²⁰For I tell you, unless your righteousness exceeds that of the scribes and Pharisees, you will never enter the kingdom of heaven."

[handwritten top margin: pray & mediat] *[handwritten: 1 poor in spirit 2 persecuted 3 righteous sake]*

FRUITS OF PRAYER

ONGOING CONVERSION

The fruit connected with the third Luminous Mystery is ongoing conversion, something that is required of all Christians.

This virtue is reflected in the last of the four stages of conversion associated with the Rite of Christian Initiation of Adults (R.C.I.A.). Those stages are the inquiry period, the catechumenate, the period of purification and enlightenment, and finally mystagogia.

The period of inquiry is intended to help a person searching for faith within the Church community. The catechumenate is a lengthy period of formation and reflection on God's Word. The period of purification and enlightenment, which often corresponds to Lent, prepares catechumens and candidates to receive the sacraments. Mystagogia is the ongoing formation required of all Christians who seek to remain integrated within the Church.

As you meditate about Jesus' proclamation of the kingdom of heaven, ask God for the virtue of ongoing conversion in order that you can avoid becoming lethargic about your faith and may instead gain the grace and strength to move closer to your goal of union with Christ.

1 In the Beatitudes listed in *Matthew* 5:3–11, two specifically mention the kingdom of heaven as a reward. According to Jesus, what are the two types of people who will receive this reward?

2 In *Matthew's Gospel*, the Beatitudes that promise the kingdom of heaven act as bookends for the collection. What rewards does Jesus attach to the six Beatitudes that fall in the middle? With which of the eight Beatitudes do you most identify, and why? Which is most difficult for you to understand or to implement in your life?

3 In *Matthew* 3:2, John the Baptist preaches: "Repent, for the kingdom of heaven is at hand," and in *Matthew* 10:7, Jesus also preaches that the kingdom of heaven is at hand. Explain what you think is meant by saying that the kingdom of heaven is "at hand." How do you think that practicing the virtues Jesus sets forth in the Beatitudes might help to further the kingdom of heaven on earth?

[handwritten: 24/7 now here + within + not in sequence element or now]

4 St. Augustine (354–430) described the kingdom of heaven this way: "There we shall rest and see, we shall see and love, we shall love and praise." When you imagine heaven, what are some of its characteristics? What reasons you can think of to explain why some people are not interested in the kingdom of heaven?

[handwritten: love friends & all family 2 answered]

5 The blessings promised by Jesus confront Christians with decisive moral choices. According to the Church, how do these choices bring about true happiness (*CCC* 1723)? Why do you think that Jesus follows his teaching about the Beatitudes with strong admonitions not to reject the law given to Moses?

[handwritten: Pure of heart → grace not speak them +]

BLESSINGS OF THE KINGDOM

While Matthew presents the Beatitudes as a series of eight blessings taught by Jesus during the Sermon on the Mount (*Matthew* 5:3–11), Luke presents similar material in a slightly different fashion as four blessings and four woes that Jesus teaches during the Sermon on the Plain (*Luke* 6:17–26).

A primary difference in *Luke's Gospel* is the insistence on blessing people who actually are poor, not just poor in spirit; who actually are hungry, not just hungering and thirsting for righteousness. The account in *Luke* also focuses on the woes that will befall those who have achieved earthly success. The account in *Matthew* instead looks at the happiness that will come to those who are sincere about seeking the kingdom of heaven.

In *Matthew* 5:17–20, Jesus also deliberately mentions the law and commandments already in place (*Exodus* 20:1–17), and he links adherence to them with entry into the kingdom of heaven.

EXODUS 19:16–20:20

16On the morning of the third day there was thunder and lightning, and a thick cloud upon the mountain, and a very loud trumpet blast, so that all the people who were in the camp trembled. 17Then Moses brought the people out of the camp to meet God; and they took their stand at the foot of the mountain. 18And Mount Sinai was wrapped in smoke, because the LORD descended upon it in fire; and the smoke of it went up like the smoke of a kiln, and the whole mountain quaked greatly. 19And as the sound of the trumpet grew louder and louder, Moses spoke, and God answered him in thunder. 20And the LORD came down upon Mount Sinai, to the top of the mountain, and Moses went up. 21And the LORD said to Moses, "Go down and warn the people, lest they break through to the LORD to gaze and many of them perish. 22And also let the priests who come near to the LORD consecrate themselves, lest the LORD break out upon them." 23And Moses said to the LORD, "The people cannot come up to Mount Sinai; for you yourself charged us, saying, 'Set bounds about the mountain, and consecrate it.'" 24And the LORD said to him, "Go down, and come up bringing Aaron with you; but do not let the priests and the people break through to come up to the LORD, lest he break down against them." 25So Moses went down to the people and told them.

1And God spoke all these words, saying, 2"I am the LORD your God, who brought you out of the land of Egypt, out of the house of bondage. 3"You shall have no other gods before me.

4"You shall not make for yourself a graven image or any likeness of anything that is in heaven above, or that is in the earth beneath, or that is in the water under the earth; 5you shall not bow down to them or serve them; for I the LORD your God am a jealous God, visiting the iniquity of the fathers upon the children to the third and the fourth generation of those who hate me, 6but showing mercy to thousands of those who love me and keep my commandments.

7"You shall not take the name of the LORD your God in vain; for the LORD will not hold him guiltless who takes his name in vain.

8"Remember the sabbath day, to keep it holy. 9Six days you shall labor, and do all your work; 10but the seventh day is a sabbath to the LORD your God; in it you shall not do any work, you, or your son, or your daughter, your manservant, or your maidservant, or your cattle, or the sojourner who is within your gates; 11for in six days the LORD made heaven and earth, the sea, and all that is in them, and rested the seventh day; therefore the LORD blessed the sabbath day and hallowed it.

12"Honor your father and your mother, that your days may be long in the land which the LORD your God gives you.

13"You shall not kill.

14"You shall not commit adultery.

15"You shall not steal.

16"You shall not bear false witness against your neighbor.

17"You shall not covet your neighbor's house; you shall not covet your neighbor's wife, or his manservant, or his maidservant, or his ox, or his donkey, or anything that is your neighbor's."

18Now when all the people perceived the thunder and lightning and the sound of the trumpet and the mountain smoking, the people were afraid and trembled; and they stood afar off, 19and said to Moses, "You speak to us, and we will hear; but let not God speak to us, lest we die." 20And Moses said to the people, "Do not fear; for God has come to test you, and that the fear of him may be before your eyes, that you may not sin."

[handwritten note:] Psalm 6

God + I are enough!
Coincidences are small miracles in which God chooses to renew anonymous.

6 *Exodus* 20:3–17 sets forth ... to Moses on Mt. Sinai. Pa... *Catholic Church* teaches that th... cations of belonging to God: "... Lord's loving initiative." Expl... ments reflects God's love for ... Church are available to those w...

[handwritten:] Penance –

7 The 10 Commandments a... the middle of a theophany, ... *Exodus* 19:16, what physical si...mandments? How do the people react to these signs?

[handwritten:] trumpet & tremble fear

8 *Exodus* 19:18 records that the LORD descended on Mt. Sinai in fire. Review Lesson 19, *A Sound Came from Heaven Like the Rush of a Mighty Wind* on pages 70–73. Explain similarities and differences between God's descent on Mt. Sinai and in the upper room.

[handwritten:] tongues of fire – dove

9 One of Jesus' titles is the new Moses, based in part on *Deuteronomy* 18:18, in which Moses promises the Israelites that God will send them another prophet like him. List all the ways you can think of that Jesus and Moses are similar.

[handwritten:] suffer pray ... taught of miracles grace healed ...

10 Why do you think that the people are frightened when God descends on Mt. Sinai? What do the Israelites fear will happen if they listen directly to God's voice? In *Exodus* 20:20, what does Moses say is the reason that God has come to Mt. Sinai? Explain whether you think that the people fear Jesus at the Sermon on the Mount.

[handwritten:] awe comfort & healed ...

GOD COMES TO MEET HIS PEOPLE

As the expression of natural law, the 10 Commandments represent humanity's fundamental duties toward God and neighbor. As the fulfillment of the law, Jesus expresses what is essential about the law—love of God and love of neighbor. Paragraph 2056 of the *Catechism of the Catholic Church,* which refers to the 10 Commandments as the "Decalogue" or "ten words" revealed by God, teaches: "[I]t is in the New Covenant in Jesus Christ that their full meaning will be revealed."

It is in love that God comes to meet his people on Mt. Sinai, to bestow on them the "ten words" that point to the conditions for life. Moses sets forth the covenantal terms: "If you obey the commandments of the LORD your God which I command you this day, by loving the LORD your God, by walking in his ways, and by keeping his commandments and his statutes and his ordinances, then you shall live and multiply" (*Deuteronomy* 30:16).

It is the same love that also motivates Jesus to go up on the mountain to teach his people what is necessary to enter the kingdom of heaven.

... connection ... and the ...nciliation, ... saints of ...version ... means ...to God's ...ewing ... a "divine force" of every reform and is expressed in a real evangelizing effort. In Confession, through the freely bestowed action of divine Mercy, repentant sinners are justified, pardoned, and sanctified, and they abandon their former selves to be reclothed in the new.

Only those who have let themselves be profoundly renewed by divine grace are able to bear within them—and hence to proclaim—the newness of the Gospel. In his apostolic letter *Novo Millennio Ineunte* (Beginning of the New Millennium), Blessed John Paul II wrote: "I am also asking for renewed pastoral courage in ensuring that the day-to-day teaching of Christian communities persuasively and effectively presents the practice of the sacrament of Reconciliation."

I would like to reassert this appeal, in the awareness that the new evangelization must acquaint the people of our time with the face of Christ as *mysterium pietatis*, the one in whom God shows us his compassionate heart and reconciles us fully with himself. It is this face of Christ that must be rediscovered through the sacrament of Penance. **"**

—Pope Benedict XVI
9 March 2011

LESSON 25

May Day 2013

THIS IS MY SON, MY CHOSEN; LISTEN TO HIM!

The Transfiguration—the event in which Jesus reveals his divine glory—occurs atop a mountain, symbolizing the spiritual heights to which humanity is called. The three disciples who are present at the time are excited to recognize Moses and Elijah, and Peter suggests that the disciples make three booths, or tents, to mark the location. At this point, God overshadows the mountain in a cloud and tells Peter, John, and James to listen to his Son. This suggests God has been prompted by the three disciples' desire to "camp out" on the mountain, that is, their urge to stay put in the contemplative realm instead of returning to everyday concerns. Which of Jesus' words have you found helpful when attempting to discern the proper balance between contemplation and action in your life?

LUKE 9:23–35

23And he said to all, "If any man would come after me, let him deny himself and take up his cross daily and follow me. 24For whoever would save his life will lose it; and whoever loses his life for my sake, he will save it. 25For what does it profit a man if he gains the whole world and loses or forfeits himself? 26For whoever is ashamed of me and of my words, of him will the Son of man be ashamed when he comes in his glory and the glory of the Father and of the holy angels. 27But I tell you truly, there are some standing here who will not taste death before they see the kingdom of God."

28Now about eight days after these sayings, he took with him Peter and John and James, and went up on the mountain to pray. 29And as he was praying, the appearance of his countenance was altered, and his clothing became dazzling white. 30And behold, two men talked with him, Moses and Elijah, 31who appeared in glory and spoke of his exodus, which he was to accomplish at Jerusalem. 32Now Peter and those who were with him were heavy with sleep but kept awake, and they saw his glory and the two men who stood with him. 33And as the men were parting from him, Peter said to Jesus, "Master, it is well that we are here; let us make three booths, one for you and one for Moses and one for Elijah"—not knowing what he said. 34As he said this, a cloud came and overshadowed them; and they were afraid as they entered the cloud. 35And a voice came out of the cloud, saying, "This is my Son, my Chosen; listen to him!"

1 Jesus' Transfiguration is recorded in all three synoptic Gospels (*Matthew* 17:1–8, *Mark* 9:2-8, and *Luke* 9:28-35). In every instance, the voice of God is heard telling the three disciples who witness the event to listen to Jesus. This suggests that Jesus' next words will be of particular importance. In each account, what are those next words (see *Matthew* 17:7, *Mark* 9:12, and *Luke* 9:41)? Synoptic means "with the same eye." Why do you think the synoptic writers all record Jesus saying different words after the Transfiguration?

2 In *Luke* 9:26-27, when Jesus speaks about the Son of Man coming in glory, he says: "There are some standing here who will not taste death before they see the kingdom of God." What do you think that Jesus means by these mysterious words? Explain whether you think they might be related to his Transfiguration.

DESIRE FOR HOLINESS

The fruit associated with the fourth Luminous Mystery, the Transfiguration, is the Desire for Holiness.

The closer Christians get to Jesus, the more they want to be like him. Peter, James, and John are depicted as Jesus' closest friends. They are with Jesus at the raising of Jairus' daughter (*Mark* 5:35-43), at the Transfiguration, and at Jesus' agony in the Garden of Gethsemane (*Mark* 14:32-42). On Mt. Tabor, they are given a glimpse of Jesus' glory to strengthen their faith.

St. Gregory of Nyssa (335–395) likened the spiritual life to climbing a mountain: "He who climbs never stops going from beginning to beginning, through beginnings that have no end. He never stops desiring what he already knows."

If you struggle to embrace difficulties and have trouble recognizing them as opportunities to grow in holiness, a good place to start is to ask God for the desire to be holy. Christians who keep their eyes fixed on Jesus—like the disciples with Jesus at the Transfiguration—will find that the Holy Spirit gives them strength to embrace their difficulties with joy and courage.

3 In *Luke* 9:28–29, what is Jesus doing at the time when his countenance is altered? Why do you think that Jesus asks Peter, John, and James to accompany him when he goes up on the mountain?

4 In *Luke* 9:30–31, Moses and Elijah, traditional representatives of the law and the prophets, appear at Jesus' Transfiguration. Read *Deuteronomy* 18:15–16 and *Malachi* 4:4–6. Explain how these passages support the Jewish belief that these Old Testament figures would reappear before the arrival of the Messiah. *Luke* 9:31 uses the word "exodus" to refer to Jesus' forthcoming Passion, death, and Resurrection. Why do you think that this might be a fitting term?

5 Why do you think that Moses and Elijah show up to discuss Jesus' exodus with him? How does Jesus' exodus resemble the Old Testament exodus in which Moses led the Israelites out of Egypt (see *Exodus* 14:1–29)? Explain how Elijah's passing into heaven bears similarities to the original exodus (refer to Question 9 in *Why Do You Stand Looking Into Heaven?* on page 69).

GLORY FROM ON HIGH

In the Transfiguration, Jesus reveals his glory to three of his chosen disciples. Paragraph 555 of the *Catechism of the Catholic Church* teaches that divine glory mysteriously is tied to the way of the cross: "Moses and Elijah had seen God's glory on the Mountain; the Law and the Prophets had announced the Messiah's sufferings." Earthly glory is associated with honor and splendor, but heavenly glory comes at a price. While the Transfiguration provides a foretaste of the glory to which all Christians are called, *Acts* 14:22 recalls that it is through "many tribulations" that men and women are able to enter the kingdom of God.

This only is possible because of Jesus' supreme sacrifice. Paragraph 705 of the *Catechism of the Catholic Church* points out that humanity is disfigured by sin and death, remaining "'in the image of God,' but deprived "of the glory of God,' of his 'likeness.'" This highlights the often-overlooked link between God's glory and his likeness. "The promise made to Abraham inaugurates the economy of salvation, at the culmination of which the Son himself will assume that 'image' and restore it in the Father's 'likeness,' by giving it again its Glory, the Spirit who is 'the giver of life.'"

In addition, paragraph 705 clearly equates the restoration of God's likeness with God's glory, that is, with the gift of "the Spirit who is 'the giver of life'." Jesus Christ, through his sacrificial death, is able to bring about the union of humanity (God's Creation) and divinity (the eternal life of the Blessed Trinity). The Transfiguration points toward humanity's entrance into eternal glory.

EXODUS 34:29–35

²⁹When Moses came down from Mount Sinai with the two tables of the covenant in his hand as he came down from the mountain, Moses did not know that the skin of his face shone because he had been talking with God. ³⁰And when Aaron and all the sons of Israel saw Moses, behold, the skin of his face shone, and they were afraid to come near him. ³¹But Moses called to them; and Aaron and all the leaders of the congregation returned to him, and Moses talked with them. ³²And afterward all the sons of Israel came near, and he gave them in commandment all that the LORD had spoken with him in Mount Sinai. ³³And when Moses had finished speaking with them, he put a veil on his face; ³⁴but whenever Moses went in before the LORD to speak with him, he took the veil off, until he came out; and when he came out, and told the sons of Israel what he was commanded, ³⁵the sons of Israel saw the face of Moses, that the skin of Moses' face shone; and Moses would put the veil upon his face again, until he went in to speak with him.

6 In *Luke* 9:32, what difficulty threatens to prevent Peter, John, and James from witnessing Jesus' Transfiguration? How do you suppose these three disciples are able to recognize that Moses and Elijah are the ones talking with Jesus?

7 In *Luke* 9:33, Peter comes up with the idea of building three booths (or shelters) on the site where the Transfiguration has occurred. What does Peter's suggestion indicate about the relative importance that he places on the law (represented by Moses), the prophets (represented by Elijah), and the Messiah (Jesus)? What phrase in *Luke* 9:33 indicates that Peter's understanding is flawed, and what do you think might be the flaw in Peter's thinking?

8 In addition to speaking from a cloud at Jesus' Transfiguration, at what other event in Jesus' life did God speak from heaven in an audible voice (see *Matthew* 3:17, *Mark* 1:9–11, *Luke* 3:21–22, and *John* 1:32–34)? With what major Old Testament event is the voice of God most associated (see *Genesis* 1:1–31)? Explain how Jesus also is associated with that Old Testament event (see *John* 1:1–3).

9 In the *Letter to the Colossians* 3:3–4, St. Paul writes of a life hidden in God. Through which sacrament do Christians enter this hidden life? According to Church teaching, when will Christians also appear with the risen Christ in glory (see *CCC* 1003)?

10 *Exodus* 34:29–35 records that Moses's face shone when he came down from Mt. Sinai because he had been talking with God. What kind of relationship does Moses have with God (see *Exodus* 33:11)? Explain whether you think that it is possible for anyone else to develop that kind of relationship with God. What do you think such a relationship might entail, and would it be worth it?

MOSES' SHINING FACE

Because the Israelites were afraid to come near Moses after he had been talking with God, Moses developed the habit of veiling his shining face.

From God's first words at Creation—"Let there be light" (*Genesis* 1:3)—to the final book of the New Testament in which Jesus identifies himself as "the bright morning star" (*Revelation* 22:16), images of light accompany the presence of God. In religious art, Jesus often is shown with a halo, and circles of light are used with artistic depictions of the saints to represent their close association with divinity.

As people become more holy (more like God), they begin to reflect the source of that holiness. In the Old Testament, God's glory is seen on Moses' shining face; in the New Testament, Moses appears in glory at the Transfiguration.

TAKE, EAT; THIS IS MY BODY

The Institution of the Eucharist, the fifth Glorious Mystery of the Rosary, is recorded in the synoptic Gospels (*Matthew* 26:26–29, *Mark* 14:22–25, and *Luke* 22:14–20) and by St. Paul (*1 Corinthians* 11:23–26). Only *Luke's Gospel* and the *First Letter to the Corinthians* include Jesus' specific instruction that the disciples remember and repeat this shared meal of bread and wine.

The language of remembrance is linked to the Old Testament liturgy of the Passover (*Exodus* 13:3–10), as well as to the third of the 10 Commandments given by God to Moses on Mt. Sinai: "Remember the sabbath day, to keep it holy" (*Exodus* 20:8). It should come as no surprise that in instituting the Eucharist Jesus says: "Do this in remembrance of me" (*1 Corinthians* 11:24).

Think about events of your life that you regularly celebrate. How many are related to religious practices? Why do you think God asks men and women to rely on the use of memory as a foundation for worship? Describe a time when you found the Eucharist especially moving and memorable.

MATTHEW 26:26–29

[26]Now as they were eating, Jesus took bread, and blessed, and broke it, and gave it to the disciples and said, "Take, eat; this is my body." [27]And he took a chalice, and when he had given thanks he gave it to them, saying, "Drink of it, all of you, [28]for this is my blood of the covenant, which is poured out for many for the forgiveness of sins. [29]I tell you I shall not drink again of this fruit of the vine until that day when I drink it new with you in my Father's kingdom."

1 Paragraph 1324 of the *Catechism of the Catholic Church* reinforces that the Eucharist is the source and summit of Christian life by teaching: "The other sacraments … are bound up with the Eucharist and are oriented toward it. For in the blessed Eucharist is contained the whole spiritual good of the Church, namely Christ himself.…" What are the other six sacraments of the Church (see *CCC* 1113)? Explain how Jesus Christ is present in each of these sacraments and how each sacrament is oriented toward the Eucharist.

2 Read *Genesis* 14:17–24, which records Abraham's meeting with Melchizedek (although Abraham still is called Abram at this point in Scripture). What two important offices are held by Melchizedek? Who is Abraham, and why is he considered a significant Old Testament figure by both Jews and Christians (refer to *God the Father: Creation and Faith* on pages 10–13)?

3 *Genesis* 15:1–21 records the account of God entering into covenant with Abraham. What covenantal promises does God make to Abraham? Explain whether you think that the timing of God entering into this covenant with Abraham is in any way tied to Abraham's meeting with Melchizedek.

WATER TO WINE, WINE TO BLOOD

In a sign that launches his ministry, Jesus turns water to wine at the wedding in Cana (*John* 2:1–11). Before his Passion, death, and Resurrection—which occur at the end of his earthly ministry—Jesus turns wine into his own blood, instituting the sign of the new and eternal covenant. Paragraph 1334 of the *Catechism of the Catholic Church* teaches that when Jesus institutes the Eucharist he gives a new and definitive meaning to the bread and the cup associated with the Jewish Passover meal.

4 How does the bread and wine Melchizedek offers serve as an Old Testament prefiguration of the Eucharist (see *CCC* 1333)? What do you think there is about this offering of bread and wine that sets it apart as a foreshadowing of New Testament liturgy?

5 According to *Matthew's Gospel,* which Jewish religious holiday are Jesus and his disciples celebrating when Jesus institutes the sacrament of the Eucharist (see *Matthew* 26:17 and *CCC* 1339)? Which major Old Testament event does this holiday commemorate?

6 Read *Exodus* 12:1–32, the account of the tenth plague that God sends against the Egyptians. How does the slaying of a lamb protect the Israelites? Read *John* 1:29. How do you think that John the Baptist is able to recognize Jesus as the "Lamb of God"? According to Church teaching, how does Jesus' Paschal sacrifice allow for the redemption of humanity (see *CCC* 613)? How is salvation of Christians similar to the way that God saved the Israelites from death?

THE PASCHAL MYSTERY

The book of *Exodus* recounts the story of the Israelites' deliverance from slavery in Egypt and their wandering in the wilderness. After 40 years they finally reach the Promised Land, the name given to the land of Canaan because God made a covenantal promise to give it to Abraham's descendants.

The fate of the chosen people completely rests in God's hands, and nowhere is this more apparent than when God unleashes a string of 10 plagues against the Egyptians in order to pressure Pharaoh to allow the Israelites to leave. The tenth plague is the most terrible, and in it God slays the first-born of all of the Egyptians, including Pharaoh's own son. The Israelites, however, are spared from the effects of this plague when death literally passes over their homes, which they have been told to mark with the blood of a sacrificial lamb (*Exodus* 12:1–32). The Jewish feast of the Passover is instituted as a perpetual liturgical commemoration of this event (*Exodus* 13:3–10).

Paragraph 1340 of the *Catechism of the Catholic Church* teaches that Jesus "fulfills the Jewish Passover and anticipates the final Passover of the Church in the glory of the kingdom."

Jesus does this shedding his own blood, the same way that the blood of the Passover lamb was shed and used to mark the dwelling places of God's chosen people prior to their original exodus out of Egypt. John the Baptist goes so far as to identify Jesus as the "Lamb of God, who takes away the sin of the world!" (*John* 1:29). Death now can "pass over" all men and women who have been redeemed by the sacrificial blood of Jesus.

FRUITS OF PRAYER

EUCHARISTIC DEVOTION

The fifth Luminous Mystery is paired with the virtue of Eucharistic devotion. This profound dedication is a response to the love of Jesus Christ poured into the hearts of Christians through the Holy Spirit. Men and women receive this love in the sacrament of Baptism, it is strengthened at Confirmation, and it is nourished through full and active participation in the Liturgy of the Eucharist.

Paragraph 1324 of the *Catechism of the Catholic Church* teaches: "The Eucharist is the source and summit of the Christian life." Translated into action, Eucharistic devotion means never missing a Sunday Mass without a serious reason. It means participation in daily Mass whenever possible.

Eucharistic devotion can mean spontaneously stopping at a Catholic church to pray before the tabernacle, or it can mean spending a regular hour in Eucharistic Adoration.

It also could involve praying the Rosary. In *Rosarium Virginis Mariae,* Blessed John Paul II taught that the Rosary prayers are a continuous praise of Jesus, a contemplation of the face of Jesus through the heart of his mother.

EXODUS 16:1–15

[1]They set out from Elim, and all the congregation of the sons of Israel came to the wilderness of Sin, which is between Elim and Sinai, on the fifteenth day of the second month after they had departed from the land of Egypt. [2]And the whole congregation of the sons of Israel murmured against Moses and Aaron in the wilderness, [3]and said to them, "Would that we had died by the hand of the LORD in the land of Egypt, when we sat by the fleshpots and ate bread to the full, for you have brought us out into this wilderness to kill this whole assembly with hunger.

[4]Then the LORD said to Moses, "Behold, I will rain bread from heaven for you; and the people shall go out and gather a day's portion every day, that I may test them, whether they will walk in my law or not. [5]On the sixth day, when they prepare what they bring in, it will be twice as much as they gather daily." [6]So Moses and Aaron said to all the sons of Israel, "At evening you shall know that it was the LORD who brought you out of the land of Egypt, [7]and in the morning you shall see the glory of the LORD, because he has heard your murmurings against the LORD. For what are we, that you murmur against us?" [8]And Moses said, "When the LORD gives you in the evening flesh to eat and in the morning bread to the full, because the LORD has heard your murmurings which you murmur against him—what are we? Your murmurings are not against us but against the LORD."

[9]And Moses said to Aaron, "Say to the whole congregation of the sons of Israel, 'Come near before the LORD, for he has heard your murmurings.'" [10]And as Aaron spoke to the whole congregation of the sons of Israel, they looked toward the wilderness, and behold, the glory of the LORD appeared in the cloud. [11]And the LORD said to Moses, [12]"I have heard the murmurings of the sons of Israel; say to them, 'At twilight you shall eat flesh, and in the morning you shall be filled with bread; then you shall know that I am the LORD your God.'"

[13]In the evening quails came up and covered the camp; and in the morning dew lay round about the camp. [14]And when the dew had gone up, there was on the face of the wilderness a fine, flake-like thing, fine as hoarfrost on the ground. [15]When the sons of Israel saw it, they said to one another, "What is it?" For they did not know what it was. And Moses said to them, "It is the bread which the LORD has given you to eat."

7 Read *Exodus* 16:1–8. What complaint do the Israelites bring against Moses and Aaron? Do you think that this is a fair complaint, given the history of Moses' and Aaron's actions in leading the Israelites safely out of Egypt? Who does Moses say that the people really are murmuring against? What test does God devise for the Israelites? What do you think might make this test difficult?

8 The bread that God sends the Israelites to eat is called manna. How long do the people subsist on manna (see *Exodus* 16:35)? Read *John* 6:22–59. Who do you think is being tested in this passage, known as the Bread of Life discourse? What are the distinctions that Jesus makes between manna in the wilderness and the bread of life that he will give? In *John* 6:60–71, who do you think is being tested? Who passes that test, and who fails it?

BREAD OF LIFE

Although *John's Gospel* does not include an account of Jesus' institution of the Eucharist, in the Bread of Life discourse (*John* 6:22–59), Jesus uses clearly Eucharistic terms to insist that he is the bread of life: "I am the living bread which came down from heaven; if any one eats of this bread, he will live for ever…"(*John* 6:51).

9 According to Church teaching, what are the fruits, or virtues, that grow out of receiving the Eucharist in Holy Communion (see *CCC* 1391, *CCC* 1393, and *CCC* 1395–1398)?

10 The five Luminous Mysteries, or the Mysteries of Light, were introduced by Blessed John Paul II to focus on key moments in Jesus' public ministry in order to shed light on who Jesus Christ is and to draw Christians closer to him. Describe one way that your understanding of Jesus has grown through studying about Scripture and the Rosary. Describe one way that your relationship with God has become more intimate as a result of increased understanding.

A PRAYER FOR ALL SEASONS

Many people designate certain days of the week for praying a particular set of Mysteries, but any Mystery or set of Mysteries may be prayed at any time. The following is one of several different schedules for praying five decades of the Rosary each day.

The Joyful Mysteries are prayed on Mondays and Saturdays, on Sundays during Advent, and on Sundays from Epiphany to Lent. These Mysteries traditionally are associated with Advent.

The Luminous Mysteries are prayed on Thursdays throughout the year. They are associated with Ordinary Time on the Church's liturgical calendar.

The Sorrowful Mysteries are prayed on Tuesdays, Fridays, and daily from Ash Wednesday until Easter Sunday. They traditionally are associated with the season of Lent.

The Glorious Mysteries are prayed on Wednesdays and Sundays throughout the year. These Mysteries traditionally are associated with the liturgical season of Easter.

> **"** My pontificate begins in a particularly meaningful way as the Church is living the special year dedicated to the Eucharist. How could I fail to see this providential coincidence as an element that must mark the ministry to which I am called? The Eucharist, the heart of Christian life and the source of the Church's evangelizing mission, cannot but constitute the permanent center and source of the Petrine ministry that has been entrusted to me.
>
> The Eucharist makes constantly present the risen Christ who continues to give himself to us, calling us to participate in the banquet of his Body and his Blood. From full communion with him flows every other element of the Church's life: first of all, communion among all the faithful, the commitment to proclaiming and witnessing to the Gospel, the ardor of love for all, especially the poorest and lowliest....
>
> [I ask everyone] to intensify love and devotion for Jesus in the Eucharist, and to express courageously and clearly faith in the Real Presence of the Lord. **"** —Pope Benedict XVI 20 April 2005

SCRIPTURE STUDY & PRAYER

Scripture allows men and women to come to know Jesus Christ. Prayerful reading of Scripture, called *lectio divina,* is a time-honored method of interacting with the Word of God, and it allows Christians to engage in a dialogue with Jesus in order to better understand who he is, what he did, and what he is asking of each one of us. Because the goal is more intimate relationship with God, prayer is essential to any dialogue that takes place. *Scripture and the Rosary* focuses on the connection between the Old and New Testaments and the Mysteries of the Rosary, so for this Bible study the prayers of the Rosary are an obvious choice. For any reading of the Bible to be fruitful, however, it is important to begin and end with prayer.

INDEX OF CITATIONS

INDEX OF CITATIONS

INDEX OF CITATIONS

TOPICAL INDEX

TOPICAL INDEX

HOW TO PRAY THE ROSARY

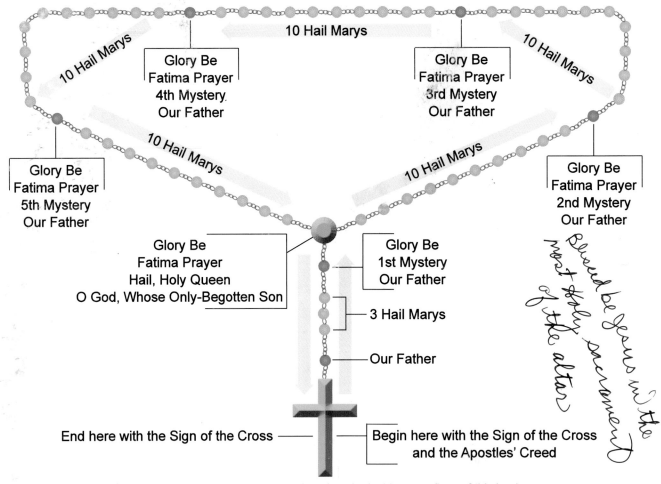

10 Hail Marys

10 Hail Marys

10 Hail Marys

10 Hail Marys

10 Hail Marys

Glory Be
Fatima Prayer
4th Mystery
Our Father

Glory Be
Fatima Prayer
3rd Mystery
Our Father

Glory Be
Fatima Prayer
5th Mystery
Our Father

Glory Be
Fatima Prayer
2nd Mystery
Our Father

Glory Be
Fatima Prayer
Hail, Holy Queen
O God, Whose Only-Begotten Son

Glory Be
1st Mystery
Our Father

3 Hail Marys

Our Father

End here with the Sign of the Cross

Begin here with the Sign of the Cross
and the Apostles' Creed

Blessed be Jesus in the most Holy sacrament of the altar

All of the Rosary prayers can be found on the inside cover flaps of this book.

*The beads converge upon the crucifix,
which both opens and closes the unfolding sequence of prayer.
The life and prayer of believers is centered upon Christ.
Everything begins from him, everything leads toward him,
everything, through him, in the Holy Spirit, attains to the Father.*

—Blessed John Paul II, 16 October 2002

ABOUT THE PICTURES IN THIS BOOK

Scenes from the Creed and the original 15 Mysteries of the Rosary are taken from *Art of Prayer*, a book featuring photographs by Tom Knapp of more then 85 stained glass panels designed by artist Charles J. Connick. The panels make up the windows of St. Augustin Catholic Church in Des Moines, Iowa.